U.S. Relations with Latin America during the Clinton Years

T0003125

UNIVERSITY PRESS OF FLORIDA

Florida A&M University, Tallahassee
Florida Atlantic University, Boca Raton
Florida Gulf Coast University, Ft. Myers
Florida International University, Miami
Florida State University, Tallahassee
University of Central Florida, Orlando
University of Florida, Gainesville
University of North Florida, Jacksonville
University of South Florida, Tampa
University of West Florida, Pensacola

U.S. Relations with Latin America during the Clinton Years

Opportunities Lost or Opportunities Squandered?

David Scott Palmer

University Press of Florida
Gainesville/Tallahassee/Tampa/Boca Raton
Pensacola/Orlando/Miami/Jacksonville/Ft. Myers

Copyright 2006 by David Scott Palmer

11 10 09 08 07 06   6 5 4 3 2 1

A record of cataloging-in-publication data is available from the Library
of Congress.

ISBN 0-8130-3017-X

The University Press of Florida is the scholarly publishing agency
for the State University System of Florida, comprising Florida A&M
University, Florida Atlantic University, Florida Gulf Coast University,
Florida International University, Florida State University, University
of Central Florida, University of Florida, University of North Florida,
University of South Florida, and University of West Florida.

University Press of Florida
15 Northwest 15th Street
Gainesville, FL 32611-2079
http://www.upf.com

For Diane

Contents

Tables

Preface

President Bill Clinton and his administration are memorable in many ways and have been widely portrayed in print, with good reason. The Clinton years spanned most of the 1990s, a time of dramatic change both at home and abroad. Clinton himself was the consummate politician, with keen instincts, extraordinary energy and charisma, and a remarkable ability to master the details of even the most complex issues. He evoked passionate support among his many admirers and equally passionate opposition among his numerous detractors. He was the first president to preside over almost six years of sustained economic growth and the only twentieth-century president to face—and survive—impeachment.

Even though his interests and experience before assuming the presidency focused almost exclusively on domestic affairs, Clinton also demonstrated on many occasions the ability to grasp quickly and comprehensively the complexity of U.S. concerns abroad. When it came to Latin America, however, he seemed to have less interest, even though his arrival at the White House in January 1993 coincided with a particularly propitious opportunity for the United States in the region. In the early post–cold war period, with elected governments in place in most Latin American countries, and with a majority of these committed to economic liberalization and market reforms, the region's goals and aspirations converged more closely with those of the United States than they had in several decades. Furthermore, his predecessor, George H. W. Bush, had overseen a set of policy departures for Latin America on which his administration could build.

With a few exceptions, however, such as the ratification of the North American Free Trade Agreement and the organization of the historic Summits of the Americas, President Clinton and his colleagues failed to seize the moment to build and sustain an effective Latin American policy around the opportunities available in the early 1990s. By the time Clinton left office eight years later, United States–Latin American relations were largely adrift, and the openings once present had closed. For those of us who follow U.S. policy toward Latin America, such an outcome was both puzzling and disturbing.

This study sets out to explain why. To do so, it places the Clinton years within the larger context of United States–Latin American policy since World War II and the more immediate context of the George H. W. Bush administration. This background makes it possible to appreciate the significance of the historical moment that greeted President Clinton upon taking office. It then proceeds to offer a broad overview of Clinton administration policies and follows with several case studies of success and failure. Finally, it assesses the degree to which progress did or did not take place within the major stated policy objectives of the administration, with longitudinal data that measure various indicators of these objectives.

The book is not intended to present an insider's view of the inner workings of the Clinton administration's Latin American policy. Neither does it try to lay out the details of the entire range of initiatives and approaches. The goals, rather, are twofold. One is to provide a broad-brushed portrait and assessment of administration policy concerns in the region. The other, complementary to the first, is to explore in greater detail several specific cases of policy for additional insights into process and outcome. Throughout, the concern is with finding elements of an answer to the question of why the Clinton administration, in spite of some successes, was generally unable to achieve its policy objectives in Latin America.

Important sources for assessments of the strengths and weaknesses of the Clinton administration are about 50 individual interviews and group discussions with career officials and political appointees involved at the time in the Latin American policy process, as well as with a number of scholars and other close observers of the policy scene. I am most grateful for the willingness of each of those who met with me to share experiences and views at length and with great candor, even with the knowledge that my goal was to write a book on the Clinton administration's Latin American policy. Some I had known for years, dating back to my work at the State Department's Foreign Service Institute or over the course of my college and university teaching; others I was meeting for the first time. Whatever our prior relationship, each offered insights and anecdotes that combined to enhance significantly both my understanding of policy and process and the quality of the analysis. Put simply, this book could not have been written without their input.

The result, the first book-length overview of Latin American policy during the Clinton years, is intended for scholars and students of foreign and regional policy, members of the foreign affairs community, and interested citizens. It uses a constraints approach to suggest the degree to which U.S. foreign policy in general and Latin American policy in particular were affected by a variety of bureaucratic, resource, domestic, and leadership factors, as well as unanticipated events, that often limited its effectiveness. While scholarly in its treatment, the book is written by one who has served in both academic and policy community positions, which I hope results in a presentation and analysis of the subject that is clear and understandable to all readers.

The opportunity provided by the Inter-American Dialogue for me to come to Washington as a visiting scholar there in 2001–2002 offered an ideal venue to pursue the project. The Dialogue's president, Peter Hakim, and his colleagues, particularly Michael Shifter and Ambassador Viron P. "Pete" Vaky, provided a welcoming setting as well as the impetus for two gatherings of former Clinton administration officials and interested observers to engage in wide-ranging discussions of Latin American policies. Residence at the Dialogue also greatly aided me in my ability to conduct individual interviews in the Washington area, in spite of the calamitous events of September 11 and their impact on all of us. Dialogue staff, particularly Joan Caivano, Katherine Anderson, and Rebecca Trumble, helped in many ways with the details of my stay.

Even with the assistance of the Inter-American Dialogue, the actual writing needed the additional stimulus of a number of individuals and institutions. Christine Wade of Washington College and Phil Brenner of American University put together a panel on U.S. policy at the 2004 Latin American Studies Association (LASA) meeting in Las Vegas and invited me to participate. Here I presented a paper with my initial analysis of the topic. In the discussion that followed, I received constructive critiques from fellow panelists, particularly Larry Storrs of the Congressional Research Service and Bob Pastor of American University, which helped to sharpen my focus for the larger study. Amy Gorelick, the acquisitions editor at the University Press of Florida, saw something she liked in the paper and tracked me down to see if I would be interested in expanding it into a book for her press. Boston University granted me a semester leave, making it possible to complete the manuscript.

Others who assisted in the book's preparation include Michael Williams, staff assistant in the Department of International Relations, who helped with many of the technical details, as did my teaching fellow, Deniz Gungen, Ph.D. candidate in the Department of Political Science. Katie Urbanic, my graduate assistant and M.A. candidate in the joint International Relations/ Communications Program, cheerfully tracked down any number of valuable references. Several graduate students in my Fall 2005 seminar on United States–Latin American relations, particularly Anne Delessio-Parsons and Adriana Schmidt, offered valuable comments on the draft manuscript. My wife, Dr. Diane Palmer, Massachusetts coordinator for the Center for Civic

Education, put her formidable editing skills to work to fine-tune everything I wrote, which significantly improved the final product.

For the errors and omissions that remain, I alone am responsible. Without everyone's assistance, however, this book could never have been written. Each of you has my deep and enduring appreciation.

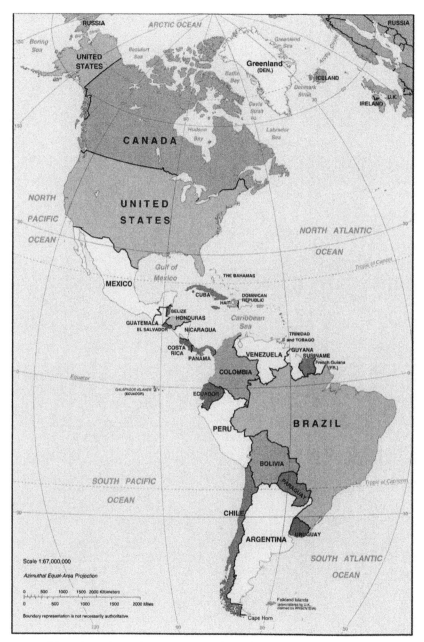

Map of North and South America. Office of the Geographer, U.S. Department of State.

Clinton's Latin American Policies in Context

The Concerns and the Approach

President William Jefferson Clinton took office in January 1993 amid major changes in the international arena. The Soviet Union was no more. The cold war had ended. Communism as an ideological alternative to capitalism had become an anachronism in full retreat. With the demise of the dominant international paradigm of bipolar rivalry that had framed U.S. foreign policy since the 1940s, new opportunities for the United States had opened up in much of the world and particularly so in Latin America.[1]

A set of equally momentous changes had swept through almost every country in Latin America. Between 1978 and 1991, 15 Latin American nations turned to or returned to electoral democracy, abandoning the authoritarian regimes that had dominated the region for some 25 years. Such a political shift was unprecedented in Latin America's long political history, which dates from the independence movements of the early 1800s.[2] At the same time, the elected leaders of many of these new democracies abandoned state-led economic models to embrace market-oriented economic liberalization based on principles of free trade and private investment.[3] Such historic changes in the region reinforced those taking place around the world and provided additional incentives for the United States to make significant adjustments in its policies toward Latin America.

As President Clinton (1993–2001) began his administration, there were ample grounds for optimism in inter-American relations. His predecessor, George Herbert Walker Bush (1989–93), had responded to the new possibilities that were opening up in the region by pursuing several policy initiatives that departed from past practices. These included free trade area negotiations with Mexico, foreign debt restructuring and forgiveness initiatives, multilateral support for protecting the new democracies, and regionally coordinated counter-drug policies. In various ways, the Clinton administration continued or built on these policy departures and in others set its own stamp on Latin American policy.

One of the Clinton administration's important accomplishments was its ability to see through to ratification the 1993 North American Free Trade Agreement (NAFTA), which had been largely negotiated by the Bush administration. Another was to hold in Miami in late 1994 the first gathering of the heads of state of Latin America and the Caribbean in almost 30 years, which was also the first meeting ever of democratically elected leaders. This Summit of the Americas (SOA) included an ambitious political, social, and economic agenda subscribed to by all attendees. The initial gathering began a process of regular hemisphere heads of state meetings, starting in April 1998 in Santiago, Chile, that have continued to the present.

U.S. officials during the Clinton years also responded effectively to such unanticipated events as the Mexican peso crisis in December 1994 and the outbreak of a border war between Peru and Ecuador in early 1995. Largely behind the scenes, U.S. efforts to assist in the resolution of a long-standing guerrilla war in Guatemala in 1995 and to help Mexican authorities open up the democratic process there between 1994 and 2000 made important contributions to conflict resolution and free and fair elections.

However, such achievements were offset by a number of failures during the Clinton years. The administration was unable to build on the success of NAFTA to expand a free trade area to other parts of the hemisphere, one of its major objectives as well as a primary goal of its Latin American counterparts. It made a disastrous miscalculation in an abortive attempt to restore democracy to Haiti in 1993 when it prematurely withdrew a U.S. ship carrying a small multilateral peacekeeping force. Although a year later there followed a U.S.–led but United Nations–sanctioned military intervention, with significant economic assistance, these efforts failed to achieve the Clinton administration's goal of restoring a working democracy in Haiti.

On Clinton's watch, in addition, democracy in Colombia and Peru was significantly eroded, in part due to the emphasis on counter-drug policies in both countries. Due to events, as well as to pressures from Congress and lobbyists, the administration also failed in its goal to gradually open up relations with Cuba. Furthermore, a reinvigorated U.S. involvement in international environmental forums and treaties as well as a regularly asserted commitment to protect and improve the hemisphere's environment were not matched by sufficient actions to stem the continuing erosion of environmental quality in Latin America between 1990 and 2000.

On the whole, then, the Clinton administration found itself unable to make significant progress on most of its policy objectives. These objectives, first formally and publicly articulated in the 1994 Miami SOA, focused on four major goals: (1) deepening democratic practice, (2) achieving economic growth and improved income redistribution within market economies, (3) eliminating poverty and discrimination, and (4) securing environmentally sustainable development.[4]

Democratic forms remained in place in Latin America throughout the 1990s, but most assessments concluded that the overall quality of democracy had declined.[5] The shift to more market-oriented economies contributed to significant increases in trade and investment and net economic growth for the decade but also produced increased inequalities between haves and have-nots.[6] The total number of Latin Americans in poverty, along with unemployment levels, actually increased slightly, even with increased social spending and greater participation by women in economic and political activity.[7] In addition, overall environmental quality in terms of deforestation and carbon dioxide production continued to decline.[8]

These general trends indicate that, over its eight years in office, the Clinton administration lost the favorable momentum for a "new" approach to United States–Latin American relations that had emerged with the historic changes in the region and the world and the largely effective policy departures of the Bush administration. There are a number of reasons that help to explain the inability of the United States to sustain and deepen many of the initial policy successes of the early 1990s. Some are contextual or related to circumstances, personalities, and events. Others are more structural in nature, the product of governmental institutions and their interactions, the relative priority of funding for domestic programs over foreign policy activities, and historical patterns.

One of the more important considerations is that President Clinton's main interest and experience related to domestic issues rather than foreign policy problems.[9] He owed his election, after all, to his ability to articulate his disagreements with his predecessor's domestic policies, particularly those related to the economy. Another is that major flare-ups in other parts of the world, from the breakup of Yugoslavia and civil war there to the challenges posed by the Soviet Union's collapse and dismemberment, often took priority over Latin American policy issues. A third is that key policy makers, including the president and his secretaries of state, had little interest in or commitment to the region. Such a lack of interest was compounded by the fact that those policy makers who were responsible for Latin America often found that they lacked the full confidence of their superiors and often received insufficient support from them, which frequently had the effect of limiting their ability to operate effectively.[10] A fourth challenge was posed by the progressive and cumulative reduction in Department of State resources. In addition to its demoralizing effect on career professionals, curtailed budgets also eroded the executive branch's institutional capacity to deal as fully as needed with the dramatic expansion in the number and complexity of foreign policy concerns during the 1990s.[11]

Another problem for the Clinton administration was the shift to a Republican-controlled Congress after the 1994 midterm elections. The new legislative opposition leaders were much more interested in domestic concerns and had a deep animus toward Clinton. The result was a significant increase in tension between the legislative and executive branches for the balance of the Clinton years.

Besides the 1998 impeachment of the president, which virtually immobilized top leadership capacity to follow through on foreign policy issues for more than a year, significant differences also expressed themselves in such specific areas as appointments, drug policy, and Cuba.[12] In addition, multiple domestic pressures also affected the priorities of the administration in the region. One major example was the tension between advancing on the counter-drug production and trafficking front, on the one hand, and enhancing democratic procedures and practices, on the other.[13]

By focusing on the contextual and structural constraints within which U.S. policy toward Latin America operated during these years, it is possible to appreciate more fully the degree to which policy makers were limited in their ability to take full advantage of the circumstances that initially favored new policy departures. Such a focus also highlights the perceptions and priorities of the leadership that operated within the rather limited space that was available, a leadership that in the Clinton years tended not to focus on the region with any consistency.

What also needs to be noted, however, is that the Clinton administration succeeded in some Latin American policy areas in spite of such limitations. This suggests that achievements are possible even when circumstances are far from optimal.

Nevertheless, the partial and even ad hoc nature of some of the successes highlights the difficulties for U.S. foreign policy in maintaining the momentum set by a previous administration, in taking full advantage of favorable circumstances, or of translating the set of Latin American policy objectives articulated at the 1994 SOA into practice. While it is necessary to explore why the Clinton administration was able to achieve some successes in United States policy toward Latin America, it is equally important to explain why it was unable to do more.

Much of the discussion below will explore why it was that, instead of seizing the favorable moment in United States–Latin American relations,

President Clinton and his foreign policy colleagues missed a historic opportunity.

A Constraints Approach

The study of foreign policy traditionally focused on an identification of the national interest and the mechanisms that could be applied to achieve it in the international arena.[14] Following this approach, the degree of success was largely determined by the nature of the international environment and the capacity of a nation to effectively use diplomacy or military action for the issue at hand to deal with the foreign actor or actors involved. With the introduction of a bureaucratic politics approach to help explain how foreign policy decisions were made and implemented, greater attention came to be focused on the policy-making process and its effect on outcomes.[15] More recently, a "two-level games" focus on international diplomacy emphasized the degree to which both domestic and international factors intertwined to explain success or failure in foreign policy.[16] Such a domestic focus for enhancing an understanding of foreign policy was subsequently formalized an a "funnel model" of the overall process that specifies the multiple components that affect and limit U.S. foreign policy making.[17]

The cumulative effect of these advances in the analysis of foreign policy has been to suggest the large number and complexity of elements that affect both its process and its outcome. They serve to highlight the degree to which a variety of constraints within the institutions responsible for foreign policy, within the domestic political arena itself, and among the variety of international actors affect both how the policy is pursued and the degree to which it is successful or not. "Policy makers are constantly playing in the domestic and international arenas simultaneously. . . . They face . . . pressures and constraints from each. . . . No longer are states the actors, rather central decision-makers, legislatures, and domestic groups become the agents."[18]

These considerations serve as the basis for the constraints approach used in this study of U.S. policy toward Latin America during the Clinton administration. This approach emphasizes the degree to which the actual space available to policy makers to carry out their foreign policy objectives is limited by multiple forces and factors. These include the bureaucratic politics of the foreign affairs agencies and departments, the interplay of domestic politics, and the role of both domestic nongovernmental as well as international actors. They also incorporate a number of other considerations that influence the decision makers' ability to conduct foreign policy, such as the impact of unanticipated events. With special reference to the United States and Latin America, they include patterns of historical relationships that have been based on imposition, a general lack of public awareness of or concern about the area, and the generally low priority accorded by key decision makers to the region.[19]

The result of the interaction of such a multiplicity of elements limits the space within which foreign policy in general, and toward Latin America in particular, can be formulated and conducted. However, such limited space also poses a constant challenge for policy makers and requires that they work diligently to bring to bear the institutions, resources, and personnel necessary to accomplish specific goals. The Clinton administration was at times able to overcome these multiple constraints to carry out effective responses to important issues. NAFTA ratification, the SOA, and the response to the late 1994 and early 1995 Mexican peso crisis were three such examples.

Where the stakes were not perceived as being as high, or where the glare of public attention was less focused, fewer contending elements were likely to be engaged. Under such circumstances, Clinton officials were less constrained and could operate more freely to achieve desired outcomes. The Guatemalan peace accords, democracy's opening in Mexico, and the resolution of the Ecuador-Peru border dispute illustrate positive policy results when such considerations were present.

Overall, however, President Clinton and his policy makers failed to exercise the decisive and consistent leadership on several important Latin American policy issues that would have increased their chances of overcoming the multiple constraints within which they operated. From not securing "Fast Track" renewal (i.e., Congress's acceptance of an up or down vote, rather than scrutinizing individual articles, once the executive branch completes negotiations on a treaty) and withdrawing the USS *Harlan County* from Haiti to signing the Helms-Burton Act and pursuing counter-drug policy at the expense of democracy, the Clinton administration succumbed to a variety of pressures that limited its ability to achieve its foreign policy goals in Latin America. In spite of some successes, then, United States–Latin American relations during the Clinton years drifted more than they developed.

Chapter Themes

To develop the exploration of inter-American relations during the Clinton years, chapter 2 summarizes the broader international, regional, and domestic historical contexts that offer the backdrop for U.S. policy toward the region in the 1990s and that serve to frame that policy. In this chapter there is a synopsis of the most significant policies pursued by the United States in Latin America during the cold war years between 1947 and 1989. The chapter also summarizes the major international and regional changes that combined to open up new possibilities for change in U.S. policy. Finally, the chapter notes the most significant policy adjustments toward Latin America pursued by the Bush administration, adjustments that offered incoming Clinton officials a new set of opportunities in the region.

Chapter 3 offers an overview of Latin American policy during the Clinton years. It provides a summary of the principal policy concerns relating to Latin America when Clinton took office; the challenges of assembling the administration's Latin American "team" during the first year; and the combination of decisive leadership, political expediency, and an often chaotic decision-making process in a variety of policy areas that came to characterize Clinton administration policy toward the region. The politically difficult decisions, for example, to push forward with the NAFTA treaty ratification and to bring together a historic meeting of Latin American heads of state in spite of opposition within the government bureaucracy, illustrate the administration's ability to make tough choices and see them through to successful completion. These contrast with such contrary examples as the failure to implement the Governors Island Accord in Haiti and the decision not to pursue renewal of Fast Track authority by Congress to facilitate future trade agreements, among others.

In chapter 4, several case studies explore the successes and failures in Latin American policy during the Clinton years and the forces at work that contributed to one outcome or another. One success is the completion of NAFTA negotiations and ratification. A second is the SOA initiative, with its extensive process of bureaucratic coordination and consultation. A third is the long and difficult but ultimately successful resolution of the region's long-standing border dispute between Ecuador and Peru.

On the other side of the ledger, one case of failure explored in some detail is Haiti, which includes both the collapse of the Governors Island Accord with the precipitous withdrawal of the USS *Harlan County* and the inability of the United States as part of the UN peacekeeping mission to achieve its objective of bringing about a working democracy in that country. A second is the failure of the Robert Pastor nomination to become ambassador to Panama, which highlights the tension between the legislative and executive branches of government and the mechanisms employed by a single senator to thwart a favorable predisposition of the majority to confirm the nomination. A third case is a discussion of the shift in policy toward Cuba with Clinton's decision to sign the Helms-Burton Act after the shooting down of the Brothers to the Rescue planes. A final case explores how the tension between two important regional policy goals—to stem drug production and trafficking and to enhance democratic practice—played out in Peru with negative consequences for democracy there.

Chapter 5 brings together the strands of the analysis in the body of the volume to provide an overall summary characterization of the Clinton administration's Latin American policy. While recognizing the commitment to the region as expressed in the articulation of overall policy objectives and an ability at times to make difficult decisions and see them through to successful outcomes, more often than not the Latin American policies of the Clinton years were limited by a variety of pressures and events and a lack of consistent presidential leadership.

The discussion focuses on the Clinton administration's four major policy goals in the region, as articulated in the Miami Summit Plan of Action, and provides the documentation in a number of tables to analyze the degree to which progress was or was not made toward achieving them. The overall conclusion is that U.S. policy during the Clinton years failed to exploit fully the opening available for expanding or deepening a new post–cold war approach, thus squandering a historic opportunity, in spite of success in specific arenas.

The chapter then summarizes the reasons noted in earlier chapters that help to explain why Clinton administration progress was so limited with regard to its overall Latin American policy objectives, as well as why it was able to succeed at times in some areas. They include both contextual and structural elements, from the level of interest and commitment and how unexpected events were dealt with to the interplay of domestic and foreign policy considerations and of executive and legislative tensions, among others. While the Clinton administration was at times able to manage these constraints, more often than not they limited its ability to act effectively.

The focus turns now to the backdrop for the Clinton administration's Latin American policy. Chapter 2 provides a broad summary of the historical context of United States–Latin American relations from the post–World War II period to the end of the cold war, and discusses the interplay of international, regional, and domestic factors and forces that shaped policy during these years.

The Changing International and Regional Context of Inter-American Relations

For more than forty years after World War II, United States–Latin American relations operated within the larger international context of the cold war and the rivalry between the United States and the Soviet Union for influence in the region. In policy terms, this meant that between 1947 and 1989, "North-South," or economic and commercial interests, were subordinated to "East-West," or security concerns. Such a national security–driven approach to the region derived from U.S. officials' fear that the Soviet Union's quest for world domination could manifest itself in Latin America through the spread of communism there.[1] If such a preoccupation seems excessive in hindsight, it was quite understandable in its historical context: Joseph Stalin's post–World War II expansion into Eastern Europe, the successful communist revolution in China, the Korean War, and the anticommunist witch hunts of the U.S. Senate Permanent Subcommittee on Investigations, led by Joseph McCarthy.[2]

During these years, the concern over the possible spread of communism in the region, bordering on obsession at times, affected the entire array of U.S. policies toward Latin America, from political institution building to economic and military assistance. With a confidence born of the successful pursuit of World War II, a new set of foreign policy instruments, and a willingness to assume international responsibilities, officials believed that they could pursue a robust and multipronged approach in the region to ensure that communism did not gain a foothold there.[3]

Democracy and Anticommunism

The U.S. commitment to democracy in Latin America, though always a stated goal of policy, took a backseat for most of the cold war to the commitment to keep communism out of the hemisphere. When conflicts between the two objectives arose during these years, democracy was often sacrificed.

The most dramatic example is the case of Guatemala in 1954. At this time, the United States abandoned its nonintervention policy, pursued since the 1930s, when the Central Intelligence Agency mounted a successful covert operation that overthrew the left-leaning but elected government of Jacobo Arbenz.[4] Another example of U.S. efforts to rid the region of what officials saw as communist threats included the failed "covert" Bay of Pigs intervention in Cuba in 1961, which had been modeled on the Guatemalan experience.[5] In addition, the U.S. military invasion of the Dominican Republic in 1965 represented a case of overt intervention during an internal conflict for political control that included some leftist elements.[6] After the victory of a left-wing party coalition led by Salvador Allende in Chile in 1970, the United States mounted both a covert and an overt campaign to undermine the government and supported the virulently anticommunist and repressive military regime when it took power in a 1973 military coup.[7]

National security concerns also underlay U.S. support for such nondemocratic governments as the Somoza family regime in Nicaragua and the Pérez Jiménez military government in Venezuela, among others.[8] Furthermore, security concerns served to justify a major expansion of CIA operations throughout Latin America that were designed to undermine the activities of Soviet-supported communist parties and labor organizations in the region.[9] At the same time, the CIA was the channel for U.S. funding to support noncommunist political parties and unions and the training of political leaders through such organizations as the Inter-American Institute of Political Education and the Institute for International Labor Research. The goal was to work with democratic leaders in Latin America, such as José Figueres of Costa Rica and Rómulo Betancourt of Venezuela, to help build a democratic alternative to communist organizations within the region.[10]

Nevertheless, U.S. commitments to support democratic practices in Latin American republics were frequently undermined when U.S. officials perceived a danger in any of these countries from communist groups. By pursuing such a policy in the region, the United States contributed to the erosion of democracy and representative institutions there and to the concomitant spread of authoritarianism in the 1960s and 1970s.

Economic Assistance and Anticommunism

The U.S. commitment to provide economic assistance to alleviate poverty was based on the rationale that U.S. resources for infrastructure, education, and health would benefit less privileged Latin Americans and simultaneously decrease support for communist groups because policy makers viewed poverty as an incubator for extremism. To pursue this view, the Point Four Program of the International Cooperation Administration (1949–60) and the Alliance for Progress (1961–70) together provided more than $26 billion in economic assistance for a variety of such programs.[11] Their successor, the United States Agency for International Development (USAID), continued economic aid to Latin America in the 1970s and 1980s with almost $12 billion over the two decades, which was about 59 percent of total U.S. economic grants and credits to the region ($19.8 billion) during these years.[12]

Whatever the rationale, the beneficial effects of these major economic assistance programs on substantial numbers of Latin American citizens were significant indeed. In combination with resource and institutional support from Latin American governments, tens of millions of citizens in the countries of the region were able to gain access to education and health services for the first time, as well as to farm-to-market roads, potable water, and improved agricultural practices. Between 1950 and the early 1990s, levels of literacy in Latin America more than tripled, as did the proportion of population receiving basic medical care, while infant mortality rates were cut in half and the proportion of the population at different levels of education increased dramatically: a fivefold increase at the primary level, sixteenfold at the secondary level, and more than thirtyfold at the university level.[13] These changes in levels of individual welfare had salutary effects on the ability of many hitherto marginalized from national societies to participate in national economic and political affairs for the first time.

The combination of increased capacities and growing involvement in national affairs induced popular expectations of further improvements in well-being. These changes, in turn, produced both a growing willingness and a greater organizing ability to pursue newfound aspirations in a reinforcing and cumulative cycle.[14] Such significant changes over the course of little more than a generation induced a variety of new pressures from below on governments, pressures to which officials too often could not or would not respond effectively.[15]

The frustrations generated by inadequate or even repressive responses were at times exploited by dissident political actors with their own antigovernment agendas and produced a progressive radicalization of social forces that in some cases included the initiation of guerrilla activity, often with the support of Cuba's communist government. Thus, one of the unintended consequences of significant improvements in the welfare of previously excluded segments of society through major infusions of U.S. economic assistance was the creation of new, often destabilizing actors by the 1960s. This dynamic contributed to a significant increase in both political violence from below and repression from above in many countries in the 1970s and 1980s.

Military Assistance and Anticommunism

The U.S. commitment to provide various forms of military assistance and training was designed to professionalize the armed forces of Latin America and to make them better able to protect their governments against external or internal threats posed by international communism. From the U.S. perspective, the goal of a more professional military included not only a greater technical capacity but also subordination to civilian political authority. Between 1947 and 1967, the United States was the sole supplier of military equipment and training in the region, and it retained its dominant position in this policy arena until the mid-1970s.[16]

Training programs ranged from two-week specialized courses for noncommissioned military personnel to yearlong immersions for prospective general officers at the School of the Americas in the Panama Canal Zone, at military bases and schools in the United States, and in the host countries. Between 1950 and 1975, some 71,651 Latin American military personnel participated in one or another of these programs.[17] The Military Assistance Program (MAP) and Foreign Military Sales (FMS) accounted for the bulk of U.S. military support for its Latin American counterparts between 1946 and 1975, totaling about $1.6 billion in all.[18] While such U.S. military support to Latin America is considerably less than that provided to most other regions of the world during the same period, it is clear that the United States played a significant role in strengthening the military institutions of most Latin American countries by the 1960s.

Stronger military institutions in the region included such elements as greater operational capacities, better equipment, more merit-based promotion procedures, and a more professional officer corps.[19] At the same time, however, the U.S. training and assistance provided and the close military-to-military relationships developed over these years did not achieve U.S. policy objectives. In many cases, the beneficiaries used their improved military skills for political purposes, such as coups against civilian governments. In the 1960s and 1970s, there were 37 such unconstitutional takeovers in 13 of the 20 Latin American republics.[20] Far from becoming a bulwark of support for democracy, most U.S.–trained Latin American militaries subverted it.

On balance, the overall result of these core elements of the security-driven foreign policy of the United States in Latin America was to produce exactly what the policy was intended to avoid—a significant increase in internal conflict, a dramatic decline in democratic procedures and practice, and a proliferation of governments that were hostile to the continued expansion of U.S. trade and investment and often to economic or military assistance as well. Clearly, the U.S. approach to Latin America between the 1940s and the 1970s was not able to deal effectively with major issues facing the region in spite of a major transfer of resources.

In various ways, then, U.S. policy actually contributed to political destabilization and social unrest. Outside actors, particularly the Soviet Union and Cuba, at times exploited these outcomes to their advantage.

Central America is a good case in point. Cuban-trained guerrilla groups emerged in Guatemala, Nicaragua, and El Salvador in the 1960s; they were able to survive government efforts to eliminate them with large-scale military operations and return much stronger and better organized in the 1970s. The success of the Sandinista National Liberation Front (Frente Sandinista de Liberación Nacional—FSLN) in overthrowing the Somoza dictatorship in Nicaragua in 1979 offered a revolutionary model and an inspiration to other guerrilla groups in the region, particularly the Farabundo Martí Liberation Front (Frente Farabundo Martí de Liberación Nacional—FMLN) of El Salvador.

Jimmy Carter's administration (1977–81) failed to keep the Sandinista revolution on a moderate course in Nicaragua and faced in its waning days the December 1980 declaration of civil war by the FMLN in El Salvador. As a result, the incoming Reagan administration (1981–89) soon mounted a major campaign designed to overthrow the FSLN and to keep the FMLN from coming to power. To this end, it helped to create and train a counterrevolutionary force in Nicaragua that came to be known as the contras (counterrevolutionaries), and it began to provide significant military and economic assistance to the government of El Salvador against the FMLN. Over the course of the 1980s, U.S. military and economic assistance to these efforts and to the other governments of Central America totaled more than $6 billion, truly significant sums for these countries' small economies.[21]

Whether or not the U.S. role in Nicaragua and El Salvador was a significant factor in helping to end the internal conflicts in both countries remains a matter of heated debate. What is clear is that the violence and destruction associated with these efforts claimed tens of thousands of lives and hundreds of millions of dollars in damage over the course of the decade.[22]

External and Regional Change

Three major developments changed the underlying elements that had long provided the rationale for U.S. policy toward the region. The most far-reaching was the end of the cold war, beginning with the reform efforts of Supreme Soviet Secretary Mikhail Gorbachev after his succession to the leadership of the Soviet Union in 1985. However, the transformation accelerated with the fall of the Berlin Wall in 1989, the break-away of the satellite states of Eastern Europe, and the dismemberment of the Union of Soviet Socialist Republics (USSR) in the closing days of 1991. This set of remarkable changes eliminated in very short order the international bipolar system framework that had generated for so many years the security-driven policies of the United States in Latin America and elsewhere.

Another was the proliferation of democratic governments in Latin America. By the end of the transition process in 1991, the region had elected civilian leaders in every country except Cuba. Such an unprecedented historical development was the product of multiple factors. Some derived from U.S. policy. One was the focus on human rights during the Carter administration. A second was the identification of democracy with U.S. national security during the later years of the Reagan administration. A third was represented by President Bush's unilateral intervention in Panama to remove Manuel Noriega in December 1989.[23]

Although the U.S. role was a factor in some instances, the major impetus for returning to or establishing democracy in most Latin American countries stemmed from internal forces. These included the ineffectiveness of the previous authoritarian regimes as well as the courage displayed by a new generation of civilian politicians in pushing for democracy.[24] Such a rapid political transformation opened up new opportunities for collaboration, both among the governments of Latin America and with the United States.

The third major development was a severe economic crisis that lasted from the early 1980s to the early 1990s. Most Latin American governments, under authoritarian or military rule, had overreached their economic capacities in the 1970s. Their foreign debt increased from $21 billion in 1970 to $257 billion by 1983.[25] Officials significantly overcommitted their public expenditures, too often in nonproductive activities. They were further debilitated by sharply declining prices for their primary product exports in the world recession of the early 1980s.[26] Following four decades of net economic growth, Latin America's Gross Domestic Product (GDP) suffered a double-digit decline between 1982 and 1992 as well as triple-digit inflation rates.[27]

Such an extended economic crisis in virtually every country except Colombia and Chile led most of the emerging democratic governments to reconsider the Import Substitution Industrialization (ISI) model, which had contributed to economic growth since the end of the Great Depression in the mid- to late 1930s. Many of these governments turned to market-oriented reform and economic restructuring to regain their economic footing.

They were actively encouraged in their efforts by the United States and the international financial community within the parameters of the so-called Washington Consensus.[28]

There were several other developments that combined with the three discussed above to reinforce the possibilities for new departures in U.S. policy toward the region. One was the Central America Peace Plan initiated by Costa Rica's president, Oscar Arias, in 1987 after U.S. involvement in the area had been temporarily neutralized by the fallout from the Iran-Contra scandal.[29] The Arias Peace Plan, as it came to be called, offered a regionally developed alternative to the hitherto U.S.–dominated approach to end civil strife in Nicaragua, El Salvador, and Guatemala through negotiations among the conflicts' actors.

Another was the fortuitous presence of the first Latin American secretary-general of the United Nations (UN), Javier Pérez de Cuéllar of Peru. His term of office coincided with growing international support for multilateral responses to conflict resolution. Pérez de Cuéllar was receptive to requests from Arias and others for the establishment of UN peacekeeping missions in the region for the first time.[30]

Such developments were reinforced by a growing recognition by the Reagan administration during its second term that support for democracy could serve as a bulwark against communist aggression. Such acknowledgment, while it failed to alter the overall security-driven approach within Latin America, did produce some adjustments in U.S. policy in the late 1980s that reinforced democratic processes already well under way in the region.[31]

The Reagan administration's shift occurred in the context of growing domestic opposition in the United States, both within Congress and among sectors of the public, to the unilateral interventionist policies being pursued in Latin America. Opposition crystallized with the 1986–87 Iran-Contra scandal, when some U.S. officials used profits from arms sales in the Middle East to support the contra rebels in Nicaragua after Congress had suspended such assistance. One result of these revelations and the congressional hearings that followed was the end of U.S. military support for the contras and a greater willingness to consider regional and multilateral approaches in Central America.[32]

Together with the broader changes represented by the end of the cold war, the return to democracy, and the economic crisis, these developments set the stage for the significant U.S. policy adjustments toward Latin America that characterized the early years of the 1990s.

U.S. Policy Change during the Bush Administration

While some of the initial responses of the United States in Latin American policy to the new realities in international and regional arenas were evident in the later Reagan years, most occurred during the George H. W. Bush administration. In a number of ways they marked significant departures from the national security–based policy trajectory of most of the post–World War II period.

The stage for these policy adjustments toward the region was set by political developments in the United States. One was the election to the presidency in 1988 of George H. W. Bush, arguably the most experienced head of state in international affairs in modern U.S. history. Before his election as vice president under Ronald Reagan, Bush had served in such capacities as ambassador to China, ambassador to the United Nations, and director of the CIA. In formation and temperament, he represented the moderate internationalist wing of the Republican Party.[33]

Another was the early appointment and confirmation of a secretary of state, James A. Baker, who had extensive experience in both the legislative and executive branches of government, as well as a close, long-standing relationship with Bush. He was known for his capacity to work well with opponents and for his ability to delegate authority and responsibility to subordinates.[34]

A third development was the decision in the first months of the administration to name Bernard Aronson as assistant secretary of state for interAmerican affairs. Although not experienced in Latin American matters, he enjoyed the confidence of Secretary Baker and, as a moderate Democrat, could reach out to the congressional majority. Aronson also proved to be "a quick study [and] a political broker who could work with both parties, even in a polarized environment."[35]

The Bush administration built on some of its predecessor's policy adjustments. However, it also initiated programs or responded to proposals from Latin American governments that departed significantly from those of the Reagan years.

THE BRADY PLAN

A major shift was an ambitious departure from past efforts to deal with Latin America's debt problem, known as the Brady Plan, after Secretary of the Treasury Nicholas Brady. Under this plan, the United States was willing to consider debt forgiveness for the first time, as well as restructuring and rollover in concert with other lending countries, the international banking community, and the private banks.

Negotiations under the Brady Plan led to agreements with Mexico, Costa Rica, Venezuela, Uruguay, Argentina, and Brazil that included forgiveness of debt in arrears or coming due of between 28 and 86 percent.[36] Such success helped restore investor confidence in the region and provided a stimulus for the economic recovery that began in the early 1990s.

FREE TRADE AREAS

Another policy departure was the historic beginning of negotiations for a free trade area. One set was with Mexico in response to a proposal in early 1990 by President Carlos Salinas de Gotari, to which Canada would also become a party. The Mexican proposal was designed to reinforce and legitimate the economic restructuring that both Salinas and his predecessor, Miguel de la Madrid, had undertaken in the 1980s but which also attracted the interest of many other Latin American governments that were implementing internal market liberalization.[37]

In addition, the executive branch worked with Congress to secure legislative Fast Track authority to enable complex trade and investment negotiations to proceed and then be submitted to Congress for an up or down vote on the entire document.[38] With Fast Track authority in hand by May 1991, formal discussions with Mexico and Canada for NAFTA began in June, were completed by August 1992, and were signed by the leaders of the three countries in October.[39] Only ratification by their legislative bodies remained for the NAFTA treaty to enter into force.[40]

These negotiations took place in the context of the Bush administration's ambitious Enterprise of the Americas Initiative (EAI), a set of negotiated framework agreements with individual countries and subregional groups on trade, investment, privatizations, and official debt forgiveness. The Bush administration also formalized a Caribbean Basin Initiative (CBI) to expand exports from the small countries of this subregion to the United States.[41]

Such historic U.S. economic policy departures emerged within a Washington Consensus, the product of meetings among governments, private banks, and international financial institutions during the late 1980s to find ways to overcome Latin America's severe economic problems. These were attributed in large measure to the structural limitations of the ISI model that most governments of the region had pursued from the 1930s through the 1970s.

The core elements of the Washington Consensus included a reduced state role in the economy, incentives for private sector investment, and free trade to stimulate economic growth.[42] The emergence of such a shared view of the measures needed to produce new capacities for economic growth and development reinforced support for the Bush administration trade, investment, and debt initiatives, thereby increasing their chances for success.

THE ANDEAN INITIATIVE

With drug consumption problems high on the list of the U.S. public's domestic concerns, another major initiative by the Bush administration was to embark on a multilateral approach to deal with the supply side of the drug issue in Latin America. Labeled the Andean Initiative, it emerged in consort and close consultation with the governments of Colombia, Peru, and Bolivia, the production source of all the cocaine consumed in the United States, as well as a significant portion of the heroin and marijuana. After meetings of the four heads of state in Cartagena, Colombia, in early 1990, the United States committed itself to a $2.2 billion program of drug crop eradication, interdiction, and alternative development, or crop substitution.

This was the first time that a multilateral approach to the drug production and trafficking problem had been attempted. While skepticism continued over a supply-side attack on what many saw as a U.S. demand-driven problem, the Andean governments supported the initiative and worked closely with the United States on its implementation.[43]

SUPPORT FOR DEMOCRACY

Given the presence of elected governments in almost every country in Latin America by the early 1990s, a logical U.S. policy innovation was to work with these governments to find ways to protect the new democracies in the region. Responding positively to a U.S. proposal at the Santiago, Chile, meeting of the Organization of American States (OAS) in June 1991, the governments reached a historic agreement. In the Santiago Declaration, or OAS Resolution 1080, member states agreed to meet whenever there were threats to any of their democracies to decide what steps should be taken to restore them or to ensure their continuance. Given Latin American governments' long-standing opposition to intervention in their internal affairs as a fundamental principle of their foreign policy, Resolution 1080 marked a significant breakthrough.[44]

The new mechanism faced its first test within a few months, in Haiti, after the September 1991 military coup there, but was unable to meet the challenge. The application of Resolution 1080 was more successful, however, in responding to its second test, the self-coup by the Alberto Fujimori government in Peru in April 1992, when OAS members met and pressured the Peruvian regime to call early elections and restore democracy within a year.[45]

CONFLICT RESOLUTION IN CENTRAL AMERICA

Finally, the Bush administration made a number of important policy changes in U.S. Central American policy. Working closely with Congress, officials reached a bipartisan agreement with legislators on an exit strategy in Nicaragua by agreeing to provide humanitarian assistance to the contras to assist in their reintegration into Nicaraguan society or their relocation, and to support the Arias Peace Plan efforts to end conflict in the region.

The administration also supported the United Nations initiative in Central America to establish peacekeeping missions in Nicaragua and El Salvador, as well as in Guatemala, where the region's longest running guerrilla war was continuing to destroy the fabric of civil society. Through these policy shifts, the Bush administration succeeded in extracting the United States from its unilateral, military-driven approach to internal conflict and supported both regionally based and international multilateral initiatives to find common ground for definitive settlements of the conflicts.[46]

These new approaches represented significant departures from earlier policies. Less unilateral, less security-driven, and more consultative, they contributed in various ways to improve inter-American relations. Even with such important adjustments, however, the Bush administration retained vestiges of the "old" policies in some areas, such as with Panama and Cuba and with regard to environmental concerns.

EXCEPTIONS

Panama

In Panama, the United States carried out a unilateral military intervention with some 24,000 troops in December 1989, after repeated provocations by the country's military strongman, Manuel Noriega, an erstwhile U.S. ally turned troublesome renegade. Noriega directed repeated harassments of U.S. military personnel still stationed in the country under the transition

terms of the 1978 Panama Canal Treaties. He was also accused of drug trafficking and illegal military equipment transfers, as well as a blatant disregard
for democratic process in Panama's May 1989 elections.

The invasion succeeded with the immediate installation as president of
Guillermo Endara, the apparent victor in the annulled elections, and with
the capture two weeks later of Noriega and his transfer to the United States
for trial on drug charges. Nevertheless, Latin American governments united
in their public condemnation of the intervention as yet another example of
the abuse of U.S. power in the hemisphere.[47]

Cuba

As for Cuba, the United States retained a hard-line policy, largely due to the
political clout of the Cuban American National Foundation (CANF) and
its leader, Jorge Mas Canosa, self-appointed spokesperson for the million-
strong Cuban American community. After some uncertainty, the Bush administration decided to support the so-called Cuba Democracy Act.

Introduced in Congress by Representative Robert Torricelli (D-NJ), the
major provisions of the legislation prohibited subsidiaries of U.S. companies abroad from trading with Cuba and required ships calling at Cuban
ports to wait six months before being allowed to dock in the United States.[48]
The administration also backed the creation of TV Martí to broadcast anti-
Castro and pro-democracy programs to Cuba, even though Cuban authorities could quite easily jam its programming. In short, domestic political considerations overrode whatever more balanced and pragmatic approaches the
Bush administration might have wished to pursue in United States–Cuba
policy.[49]

Environment

Environmental issues in the hemisphere and beyond also proved to be a
stumbling block for U.S. policy under President Bush. The "Earth Summit"
meeting in Rio de Janeiro in 1992 provided the United States with a historic
opportunity to pursue new multilateral approaches to deal with the growing problem of environmental degradation and global warming. However,
internal U.S. policy disagreements on the issue thwarted any breakthrough.
The Agenda 21 document drafted by the meeting that dealt with a wide array
of environmental concerns toward achieving sustainable development may
have been too ambitious. Nevertheless, it was concern over the document's
failure to provide adequate protection of intellectual property rights and
over the financial control given the developing countries that led the Bush
administration to reject the proposal.[50]

In spite of such exceptions, however, the main thrusts of U.S. policy toward Latin America during the Bush years responded appropriately and effectively to major issues affecting the region. Some argue that the administration came into office without any real plan for dealing with the ongoing concerns there.[51] Whether or not that was the case, by taking advantage of the openings created by the major international and regional events that occurred, U.S. policy toward Latin America shifted in significant and positive ways. These changes ushered in a relationship that could be characterized as one of pragmatism and partnership.

Now that the immediate Latin American policy context of the George H. W. Bush administration has been laid out, attention turns in chapter 3 to a broad summary overview of the major policy initiatives toward the region during the Clinton years, an analysis of the multiple challenges and constraints they faced, and an explanation for the administration's inability in most areas to build on the early successes of its predecessor.

Latin American Policy during the Clinton Years

An Overview

When Bill Clinton assumed the presidency in January 1993, there was a general consensus that United States–Latin American relations were evolving in positive and constructive directions.[1] There appeared to be a new coherence in the U.S. approach to Latin America that was based on the twin principles of support for democratic institutions and support for rebuilding market-oriented economies.

The policy goal of the former was to assist elected leaders in the region to strengthen the "new" democracies that had emerged in almost every Latin American country between 1978 and 1991. The policy objective of the latter was to overcome the region's "lost decade" of serious economic erosion in the 1980s through internal structural reform, foreign debt forgiveness and restructuring, and multilateral free trade areas. For their part, Latin American governments were on the same page as their U.S. counterparts on both principles, contributing to the most collaborative relationship between the United States and the region in several decades.

At one level, there was ample reason to expect that the incoming administration would reinforce the mostly positive policy dynamics that were already in place. President Clinton had no basic partisan or policy disagreements with most of his predecessor's initiatives. Both shared a concern for enhancing democracy, advancing peace negotiations in Central America, assisting buffeted economies to get back on their feet through debt reduction and economic restructuring, and maintaining counter-drug production and trafficking policies in the region. Even on the North American Free Trade Agreement (NAFTA), where there was significant disagreement within his own party, the president-elect committed his administration to work for its ratification with expedited labor and environment side agreements that he hoped would mollify that opposition.[2]

The other Latin America–related concern that became an issue in the campaign was how to deal with the thousands of Haitian refugees who were fleeing a repressive military government. Candidate Clinton opposed the Bush administration's policy of intercepting would-be refugees on the high seas and returning them to Haiti or taking them to the U.S. naval base at Cuba's Guantánamo Bay. By the time Clinton took office, however, Central Intelligence Agency briefings had convinced him that a surge in Haitian migration was imminent, so he decided not to change the policy after all.[3]

Such a coincidence and convergence of perspectives between the incoming and the outgoing administrations across most Latin American issues suggested that continuity, which reinforced and deepened the pragmatism and partnership approach, would characterize Clinton's policies toward the region. Even so, other considerations entered into the foreign policy equation that affected both process and outcome.

One was the fact that Clinton owed his election to a domestic rather than a foreign policy agenda, which included commitments to restore economic growth, reduce the fiscal deficit, and pursue universal health coverage.[4] In addition, the incoming president lacked the foreign policy experience of his predecessor and had little interest in foreign affairs in general. Furthermore, he had no prior exposure to or particular concern for Latin America.

These elements may explain, in part, the failure during the transition to articulate a comprehensive approach to Latin American policy and the delays that occurred in putting into place the new administration's "team" of regional specialists. Five months after Clinton took office, the only one in place was the National Security Council representative, Richard Feinberg, one strong indication that the region was not the administration's top priority.[5] Reinforcing that view was the selection of Warren Christopher as secretary of state. Although he was an experienced hand in the management of foreign affairs, Christopher apparently viewed Latin America as "a carbuncle that he wished could be lanced so that it would go away."[6]

Domestic politics also intervened. Both the Cuban American community and Representative Robert Torricelli (D-NJ) opposed Clinton's initial nominee for the Department of State's assistant secretary for inter-American affairs, Mario Baeza, and forced Clinton to withdraw his nomination for this key appointment. In part this was because the president announced his choice without consulting with key figures in Congress or representatives of the Cuban American community.[7] Such early indications did not augur well for either a careful decision-making process or a high level of concern for most Latin American issues in the Clinton administration.

There were exceptions, however. These included the issue of NAFTA ratification and the immediate and pressing problem of how to deal with the repressive military regime in Haiti. A major component of the Haitian challenge concerned the large numbers of refugees who were attempting to flee the country. Many were spurred on by Clinton's campaign statements that he would change the Bush policy of interception and return. Another element was a major disagreement within the U.S. government, particularly within the intelligence community, over how to deal with the ousted Haitian president, Bertrand Aristide. He was seen in some official circles as unstable and antidemocratic, in spite of his dramatic electoral victory in 1990.[8] Whether he wanted to or not, then, the incoming president was going to have to deal with these inherited Latin American concerns early in his administration.

Making Difficult Decisions

Once in office, Clinton made policy decisions relating to NAFTA and Haiti that tackled these politically difficult issues head on.

HAITI

With Haiti, he decided to override official doubts about Aristide and push for the restoration of democracy there. Pressed by the Congressional Black Caucus, an important Democratic Party constituency, the president committed his administration to getting Aristide back into power and to dealing in a humanitarian way with the Haitian refugee problem.

In pursuit of these objectives, the administration supported the June 1993 United Nations sanctions on Haiti's military rulers and the efforts by UN Special Representative Dante Caputo to broker an agreement among the parties, which produced the Governors Island Accord in July. Under this agreement, the military was to leave power within three months in exchange for amnesty and the lifting of sanctions. In addition, a multilateral peacekeeping force was to be put in place in Haiti to facilitate the transition back to democratic rule, and Aristide was to return as president. From the Clinton administration's perspective, implementation of the Governors Island Accord would also resolve the refugee issue. With democracy restored, the return of the estimated 35,000 Haitians who fled the military regime's repression could be justified and the possibility of new waves of refugees would be much reduced.[9]

NAFTA

Another important decision was President Clinton's determination that he should seek early congressional ratification for the NAFTA treaty, already signed by his predecessor and the heads of state of Mexico and Canada in October 1992. Many of his closest political advisors felt that the president should concentrate first on his domestic agenda. They were concerned that the NAFTA debate would split the Democratic Party by alienating its core labor constituency and free-trade opponents such as the House majority leader, Richard Gephardt. They also feared that the ratification battle, whose outcome was by no means assured, would use up the political capital needed to win legislative battles for the administration's ambitious domestic agenda.[10]

President Clinton was not to be dissuaded, however. His negotiating team quickly forged side agreements to NAFTA on labor protection for U.S. job losses and on environmental protection standards and reached agreement with Mexico and Canada in September 1993. With the support of business interest groups and their representatives, along with generally favorable media attention, Clinton led a full-court press in October to seek ratification by Congress. The result was a narrow bipartisan victory in November, thanks to Clinton's ability to secure the support of a minority of the badly divided members of his own party. The House passed the NAFTA legislation by a 234–200 vote and the Senate by 61–38. With passage, NAFTA went into effect on January 1, 1994, thus establishing the world's second largest trading bloc after the European Union.[11] By most accounts, without Clinton's leadership and personal involvement, NAFTA's ratification would not have happened.[12]

CUBAN REFUGEES

The Haiti and NAFTA challenges were not the only Latin American issues that Clinton took on directly and forcefully. A third difficult decision concerned the issue of Cuban refugees. For over 30 years, the U.S. government had encouraged and facilitated the entry of hundreds of thousands of Cubans who were fleeing Fidel Castro's communist regime. In 1980, when pressures inside Cuba generated a large number of new potential migrants, President Jimmy Carter (1977–81) encouraged them to come to the United States. Castro turned an embarrassing domestic problem into a foreign relations triumph by allowing anyone who wanted to leave to do so. The result was the departure of some 125,000 Cubans for the United States in what became known as the Mariel boatlift, an influx that totally overwhelmed the capacity of U.S. authorities to respond and contributed to Carter's defeat in the 1980 elections.[13]

By the early 1990s, following the collapse of the Soviet Union and the withdrawal of economic support for Cuba, Cubans once again experienced great hardship and began to flee on makeshift rafts in increasing numbers.[14] These *balseros* (rafters), first hundreds and then thousands, threatened to create new problems for U.S. authorities, and Clinton concluded that something must be done. Over the strenuous objections of the Cuban American community, in August 1994 the president announced the end of the longstanding policy of preferential treatment to Cuban refugees and mandated that those who were intercepted at sea be remanded to the U.S. naval base at Guantánamo Bay. In September, U.S. officials reached an agreement with their Cuban counterparts to admit at least 20,000 Cubans per year, and a few months later they announced that any new *balseros* would be returned directly to Cuba.[15]

The larger issue of setting forth a refugee policy that did not privilege any specific community weighed more heavily with the Clinton administration than the domestic political consequences of antagonizing the Cuban American population. Furthermore, this policy departure, however controversial in some sectors, brought the approach to Cuban refugees more into line with that already being pursued for their Haitian counterparts.

MEXICO'S PESO CRISIS

A fourth important decision that illustrated Clinton's ability to make difficult Latin American policy choices concerned the U.S. response to the Mexican peso crisis of December 1994. This challenge erupted shortly after the election of Ernesto Zedillo as president of Mexico. It was due primarily to a combination of fiscal profligacy by Zedillo's predecessor, Salinas de Gotari, and political assassinations in the election campaign that together weakened public and international confidence in the Mexican economy. The result was a run on dollars during the political transition and a collapse in the peso's value.[16]

Clinton was initially hesitant to respond to President-elect Zedillo's pleas for assistance, perhaps due to the dramatic and unexpected Republican Party victory in the November 1994 midterm elections and its takeover of both houses of Congress.[17] However, by February, he had forged a response, after the new Republican majority leadership affirmed its unwillingness to provide legislative support for a financial bailout for Mexico. With the guidance of Treasury Secretary Robert Rubin, the administration offered Mexico a $20 billion loan from the Exchange Stabilization Fund by executive order and successfully worked to garner up to another $30 billion, as needed, from international financial institutions.[18]

However vital a confidence booster this support was, it proved unable to stem a short-term economic crisis in Mexico or the ripple "tequila effect" of negative economic effects in much of Latin America. Nevertheless, within a year, the massive financial assistance package got both the Mexican economy and NAFTA back on track. As a result, by January 1997 Mexico had repaid the U.S. Treasury plus $1.5 billion in interest and experienced in 1996 and 1997 the country's most rapid growth in about 20 years.[19] Clinton's appreciation of the potentially devastating economic consequences for Mexico, Latin America, and the United States itself led him to push for a rapid response in spite of the negative political effects on executive-legislative relations.

Each of these decisions—the steps to restore democracy in Haiti, pursuit of the NAFTA treaty ratification, initiatives to deal with the Cuban refugee problem, and the response to the Mexican peso crisis—reflects examples of Clinton's willingness to pursue a policy because it "was the right thing to do," whether or not it was the "politically correct" approach. Together they suggest that the president and his administration were indeed able to forge an effective policy response to several difficult issues in the region.

SUMMIT OF THE AMERICAS

Beyond such discrete responses to specific problems, the aspirations of the Clinton administration for Latin America achieved their fullest expression in the formulation of the Summit of the Americas (SOA) proposal and its realization in Miami in December 1994. As Richard Feinberg put it, "President Bill Clinton's decision in late 1993 to convene a summit of his [Western Hemisphere] counterparts . . . marked a turning point in hemispheric relations—a moment in which underlying historical currents and individual initiative converged."[20]

The outlines of this initiative were first unveiled in a speech by Vice President Al Gore in Mexico in December 1993. Although faced with bureaucratic inertia and major difficulties in organization, the summit succeeded in bringing together 33 elected heads of state in a meeting without historical precedent. The gathering served to focus both the U.S. government's and the U.S. public's attention on Latin America. In addition, it signaled the political progress made in almost every Latin American country in a very few years, and it made explicit the goal of a hemispherewide free trade area as a vehicle for economic growth and development.

While criticized by many as more show than substance, the SOA served, nevertheless, as a high-profile demonstration of the Clinton administration's commitment to the region. It also laid out a specific statement of four basic objectives for inter-American relations, as follows:

1. The preservation and strengthening of democracy;

2. The promotion of prosperity through economic integration and free trade;

3. The eradication of poverty and discrimination;

4. The guarantee of sustainable development and conservation of the environment.[21]

Although these goals expressed common and perhaps utopian aims of all elected governments of the region, they also reflected the Clinton administration's overarching policy objectives toward Latin America. As such, they can serve as one basis for assessing the degree to which the administration succeeded or fell short in its policies in the region.

With the second SOA in Santiago, Chile, in 1998, the mechanism of periodic meetings of the hemisphere's elected heads of state began to take on institutional form. Besides serving as a forum to discuss common concerns, the summits also established an implementation review group and responsible coordinators among state, nongovernmental, and regional organizations to help turn agreements into follow-up actions.[22] In the articulation and implementation of the SOAs, the Clinton administration demonstrated that it was capable of putting together a long-term, visionary, and proactive initiative in its relationships with its Latin American counterparts. This may be its single most distinctive and enduring policy legacy in inter-American affairs.[23]

Following Through on Bush Administration Initiatives

Given the Clinton administration's general agreement with many of the Latin American policy initiatives of its predecessor, it is not surprising that these continued to be pursued. They included following up on debt relief, encouraging trade and investment, working for conflict resolution, and promoting democracy.

DEBT RELIEF

The Bush administration's Brady Plan, designed to work out foreign debt relief through negotiations with individual countries and their creditors, carried on under President Clinton. The agreements in principle reached with Argentina and Brazil in 1992 were finalized. In addition, new accords were worked out with the Dominican Republic, Bolivia, Ecuador, and Peru that forgave between 45 and 79 percent of eligible debt and rolled over payment on the rest to lower and more manageable levels.[24] Such agreements in the context of important trade and market liberalization reforms contributed to the restoration of international confidence in the Latin American economies. New foreign loans from both private banks and such international financial institutions as the Inter-American Development Bank and the World Bank increased by almost 70 percent, from $443 billion in 1990 to $751 billion in 2000.[25]

TRADE AND INVESTMENT

Spurred by the Washington Consensus and NAFTA, also Bush administration initiatives, trade and investment flows between the United States and the region increased substantially. Total U.S. private direct investment expanded rapidly, from $71 billion in 1990 to $239 billion a decade later, or by about 237 percent. Overall trade volume also grew at a rapid pace, some 243 percent between 1990 and 1998 (from $110 billion to $367 billion).[26] Although about 15 percent of the increase in U.S. investment and 67 percent of the increase in overall trade in the region can be attributed to Mexico and NAFTA, virtually all of Latin America benefited from such a rapid expansion in economic relationships with the United States. While responsibility for such trade and investment expansion during the decade rested primarily with the private sector, the Clinton administration's favorable stance on both facilitated their growth.[27]

MULTILATERALISM

The Bush years had also included a new commitment by the United States to support multilateral mechanisms of the United Nations and the Organization of American States (OAS). These were seen as vehicles that could find ways to reduce and end political conflict in Central America after almost a decade of largely unilateral initiatives under President Reagan. Important successes were achieved in Nicaragua in 1990 and El Salvador in 1992 with a combination of OAS election monitoring, a resettlement program, and UN peacekeeping missions.[28] The momentum favoring multilateral resolution of political conflict in this subregion continued under Clinton, focusing now on Guatemala, where the longest running and most intractable internal conflict had been taking place since the early 1960s.

Initially, Guatemalan military leaders had voiced strenuous objections to any El Salvador–type solution in the belief that the armed forces could defeat the guerrillas by force of arms. However, their inability to do so, along with the willingness of Guatemalan civilian political leaders and guerrillas alike to use outside state and international organization actors to find points of agreement, set the stage for the introduction in late 1994 of a peacekeeping mission, the UN Mission for Human Rights Verification in Guatemala (MINUGUA).[29]

Although compromised by its role in the historic covert 1954 intervention in Guatemala and by its continuing covert relationships with the Guatemalan military, the United States played an important role in assisting with the complex and difficult peace process there. This relationship included informal contacts with guerrilla representatives, a commitment to financial support with the other members of the Paris Consultative Group of Donor Countries after a peace agreement was achieved, constant encouragement for the elected government of President Álvaro Arzú, and support for MINUGUA.[30] While the historic December 1996 peace agreement could only have been achieved by the willingness of the affected parties within Guatemala to work out their differences and the presence of the 400-member MINUGUA mission to oversee compliance, the Clinton administration played a positive and constructive role throughout the process.[31]

DEMOCRACY PROMOTION

Another way the Clinton administration followed up on its predecessor's initiatives was by promoting and protecting democracy. Continued application of the OAS Resolution 1080 mechanism was one such example. During the Bush years, the military coup in Haiti in September 1991 provoked the first effort to invoke Resolution 1080 just months after its formulation at the June OAS meeting in Santiago, but this was unsuccessful. With Peruvian president Alberto Fujimori's *autogolpe* (coup d'état against his own government) in April 1992, the OAS utilization of Resolution 1080 was more effective, securing the Peruvian government's commitment to restore democratic process within a year.[32]

Guatemalan president Jorge Serrano attempted a similar *autogolpe* in May 1993, provoking a quick OAS response as well as strong outside state opposition, including the United States. These actions thwarted the unconstitutional initiative and almost immediately restored democracy under a new president selected by the Guatemalan congress, Ramiro de León Carpio.[33] In April 1996, Paraguay faced its own democratic crisis after the head of the armed forces, General Lino Oviedo, refused to step down when he was dismissed by President Juan Carlos Wasmosy. Through prompt and vigorous responses by U.S. representatives, as well as those of neighboring countries and the OAS, the principle of civilian supremacy over the military in Paraguay was restored.[34] Through its consistent actions, either through the OAS or on its own, the Clinton administration reaffirmed its commitment to democratic principles and practice in Latin America.

A much less visible but equally important effort to encourage progress toward democracy was the administration's behind-the-scenes work in Mexico, a focus that assumed added significance with the 1994 assassinations of the Institutional Revolutionary Party (Partido Revolucionario Institucional—PRI) presidential candidate, Luis Colosio, and the PRI secretary-general, José Francisco Ruiz Massieu. The deputy assistant secretary for American republics affairs, Arturo Valenzuela, made more than 40 trips to Mexico during his two-year tenure in the late 1990s to demonstrate the administration's commitment to greater transparency and democracy there.[35]

By themselves, these efforts would probably not have been sufficient to bring about the desired result of a truly open electoral process. When combined with the Mexican government's own commitment, however, particularly the steps taken by President Zedillo during his six years in office, the outcome was historic.[36] Mexico's 2000 elections produced a truly open process, one that resulted in the first presidential victory by an opposition candidate, Vicente Fox of the National Action Party (Partido de Acción Nacional), since the consolidation of the Mexican Revolution in the 1930s.

In several important areas, then, the Clinton administration continued to implement the policy departures begun by its predecessor. Combined with the difficult decisions made early in Clinton's first term concerning NAFTA, Haiti, the Cuban and Haitian refugee problem, and the larger vision of overall objectives in inter-American relations expressed in the Miami SOA, such policy continuities appeared to reflect the retention and even an expansion of the post–cold war policy departures in United States–Latin American relations begun under George Bush.

Reacting to Events

By its very nature, foreign policy is often subject to events that cannot be anticipated but for which responses are essential. The Clinton administration was forced to deal with a number of them, and it tended to do so in ways that undermined its capacity to maintain policy coherence or its ability to achieve its policy objectives in the region.

U.S. MILITARY DEATHS IN SOMALIA

One dramatic example was the killing of 18 U.S. military personnel attached to the UN peacekeeping mission in Somalia in early October 1993. This event immediately reversed the growing U.S. commitment to multilateral initiatives to deal with political conflict in troubled countries. Coming just days before a UN-sanctioned response to enforce the Governors Island Accord to restore Bertrand Aristide to power by sending a small multilateral force to Haiti led by the United States, the Somalia tragedy could not help but affect policy makers' calculations on how best to proceed.

When the ship carrying the lightly armed force, the USS *Harlan County*, steamed into the Port au Prince harbor on October 11 and found the dock blocked and a small band of protesters demonstrating on the wharf, the decision was made to withdraw rather than risk a violent confrontation.[37] This decision scuttled the Governors Island Accord to bring democracy back to Haiti, gave democracy's opponents in Haiti a new confidence and willingness to engage in political assassination and intimidation, and humiliated both the United States and the Clinton administration.[38]

SHOOT-DOWN OF THE BROTHERS TO THE RESCUE PLANES

A second dramatic event that threw the administration's policy into disarray was the shooting down by the Cuban air force of two unarmed planes of the Cuban American Brothers to the Rescue organization in February 1996. Four airmen were killed as they attempted to shower the island with anti-Castro leaflets. Up until this moment, Clinton's policy toward Cuba, while perhaps overly sensitive in public pronouncements to domestic political considerations, had worked slowly to open up ties through expanded exile visits and trips by scholars and members of the U.S. business community. Before the incident, Clinton had opposed the Helms-Burton legislation that was intended to impose a set of drastic sanctions on commerce and investment by third countries and Secretary of State Warren Christopher had intimated the possibility of a veto.

In the aftermath of the planes' downing, however, in spite of the opposition of some of his policy advisors, President Clinton concluded that he had no choice but to sign the legislation, which he did in March 1996.[39] For all intents and purposes, the adoption of Helms-Burton, even with a proviso allowing the executive to waive implementation of its discriminatory provision concerning third country trade with and investment in Cuba, represented an abandonment of the administration's efforts to pursue a more moderate course in its relations with the Castro government.[40]

RESCUE AND RETURN OF ELIÁN GONZÁLEZ

In another unanticipated event related to United States–Cuba relations, the Elián González incident in November 1999 precipitated a crisis within the Clinton administration over how best to respond. Ten-year-old Elián had survived a crossing from Cuba to Florida in an inner tube; his mother had drowned. The U.S. government was torn between allowing him to stay with his mother's family in Miami and returning him to his father in Cuba. Massive demonstrations by the Cuban American community to keep him with his relatives in Florida immobilized U.S. decision makers for weeks.

Although Vice President Al Gore eventually came out in support of the Cuban Americans' position, after much internal debate, in April 2000 Attorney General Janet Reno ordered Elián's removal from the Miami home and his return to his father. However correct the decision in terms of international law and however courageous the Clinton administration in making that determination, it also alienated the politically important Cuban American community in Florida and almost certainly contributed to the Democratic Party's defeat in the 2000 elections.

ECUADOR-PERU WAR

In addition to the U.S. response to Mexico's peso crisis, the conflict between Ecuador and Peru was another unexpected event in the region that did produce a more felicitous outcome for U.S. policy. In January 1995, the longest running border dispute in the Western Hemisphere erupted into a war between Peru and Ecuador along a contested segment of the frontier.

Although largely off U.S. media radar screens, U.S. diplomatic and military representatives played a major role in helping to facilitate a definitive resolution of the conflict. They worked diligently for over three years within the multilateral framework of an earlier treaty between the parties (Rio Protocol of 1942) to achieve an October 1998 settlement to which both parties agreed. Given the large number of unresolved land and sea boundary disputes in the region, the breakthrough to resolution of a hitherto intractable case sent a signal to other governments that their own differences could also be worked out peacefully.[41]

With the exception of the Peru-Ecuador conflict, however, the other major external events that forced U.S. policy responses and adjustments in Latin America during the Clinton years tended to undermine the administration's stated objectives in the region. Even the response to the Mexican peso crisis, while successful on its own terms, deflected attention from the historic gathering of Latin American elected heads of state at the SOA just days before it broke out.

Certainly the argument can be made, in the face of such dramatic developments as the killing of U.S. troops in Somalia or the downing of the Brothers to the Rescue planes, that President Clinton had little choice but to change course in Haitian and Cuban policy. Nevertheless, the effect in both cases was to suggest that Clinton's policy could be subject more to situations and circumstances than to a clear sense of underlying national interests and the best approaches to achieve them.

Conflicting Priorities and Conflicted Policy Actors

The effective coordination and implementation of foreign policy in the context of multiple bureaucratic and individual actors and multiple policies as well is always a daunting task. Differences are inevitable, but their successful resolution is essential to forging a set of policies that are generally effective in responding to the main issues of concern. For a variety of reasons, such as the generally low priority that top officials accorded Latin America, their rather chaotic policy-making style, President Clinton's domestic politics focus, and serious policy disagreements among government agencies, the administration too frequently adopted policies toward the region that lacked the coherence of its predecessor.[42] Examples include responses to challenges in Haiti, Fast Track authority renewal, the drug problem in Colombia, and the tension between drug policy and democracy in Peru.

HAITI

The abrupt policy turnaround on implementing the Governors Island Accord is one such example. Key advisors were virtually paralyzed by the Somalia tragedy. Secretary of Defense Les Aspin and some of his staff had been opposed from the beginning to the deployment of U.S. forces to Haiti for military or police training. In spite of the signed agreement, high levels of distrust between pro-Aristide and pro-Cedrás groups continued to fester. Most of the U.S. intelligence community remained wary about Aristide's mental competence. Aristide himself demonstrated a great deal of ambivalence about returning without the protection of a major U.S. military commitment. Given such an unhealthy mix of elements, it is not surprising that chaos reigned at the critical moment, with a disastrous outcome for U.S. policy, at least in the short run.[43] In the aftermath of this failure, the administration reassessed the situation. Under growing pressure from the Congressional Black Caucus and provoked by the publicity generated by the hunger strike carried out by the director of TransAfrica, Randall Robinson, Clinton and his advisors took steps to ensure Aristide's return to Haiti—but a year later.

The United States supported the renewal and tightening of the UN-sanctioned embargo on trade with Haiti. Individuals connected with the military regime there were prohibited from obtaining visas to travel to the United States. In addition, with the strong backing of the administration, the UN authorized the use of "all necessary means" to restore democracy to the country. As organized violence against Haitian moderates and Aristide supporters increased in mid-September 1994, Clinton authorized a high-level visit to Haiti led by Jimmy Carter.

The mission was charged with negotiating the withdrawal of the military from power and the return of President Aristide, but it was not informed about the military intervention preparations. Discussions proceeded, but virtually in mid-conversation the parties learned that U.S. forces were en route to Haiti. This revelation seemed to be the final impetus for the military regime's decision to step down. Even then, it took some deft last-minute footwork by U.S. embassy personnel and Bob Pastor, the Carter delegation member remaining in Haiti, to ensure that armed confrontations would not take place when the U.S. military landed.[44] After an arrival that was entirely peaceful, the force of some 20,000 troops prepared the way for Bertrand Aristide's return to the Haitian presidency a month later.

Even this apparent success, however belated, was tempered by the loss of 2,000–3,000 Haitian lives during the year that passed between the withdrawal of the *Harlan County* and the landing of U.S. troops. It was also affected by Aristide's reluctance to take the economic liberalization measures he had promised that would release significant aid to help with Haiti's recovery; as a result, most economic assistance never arrived. Adding to the difficulties was the ambivalence of the Department of Defense (DOD) over the use of U.S. forces for peacekeeping, which produced an early withdrawal of the significant U.S. military contingent. The remaining UN peacekeeping forces were insufficient in numbers to be able to stem the progressive regression of the internal situation in Haiti that included growing economic erosion, political immobilism, and the return to sporadic violence.[45]

Even though democratic formalities were retained, the outcome was far from what U.S. policy makers had hoped to achieve in Haiti—a weakened and ineffective government that was progressively degenerating into a virtual failed state. The U.S. experience with Haiti illustrates the difficulties of finding a solution for a problem when U.S. policy makers are divided on the best course of action and when the presumed beneficiaries of the policy, the local elites themselves, are unwilling to find some way to work through their disagreements on behalf of their own nation. For the rest of the decade, the situation in Haiti continued to deteriorate in multiple political and economic crises, a dramatic demonstration of the limits of U.S. power to effect internal change.

FAST TRACK

Haiti is not the only example of an infelicitous policy outcome. The Clinton administration's failure to secure renewal of Fast Track legislation is another. Fast Track allowed the executive branch to negotiate complex trade treaties and gave them an up or down vote without subjecting specific provisions within them to modification. This arrangement had been in place when NAFTA was negotiated and ratified, but it was scheduled to expire in 1994. Given the administration's stated interest in continuing its predecessor's commitment to trade agreement expansion in the hemisphere and its success with NAFTA, a push for Fast Track renewal was to be expected.

As events developed, however, it didn't happen, largely due to domestic politics. The battle for congressional ratification of NAFTA, though successful, had revealed serious disagreements within the Democratic Party, particularly among organized labor. Because 1994 was a midterm election year, Clinton concluded that bringing the party together for the campaign to retain a Democratic majority on the hill was more important than retaining

Fast Track.[46] But the Republicans triumphed anyway, in a dramatic November electoral victory that gave them control of both houses of Congress for the first time since the 1950s.

Fast Track was a casualty as well. Given this doubly unfavorable context, calls rang hollow at the first SOA a month later for a Free Trade Area of the Americas (FTAA) and the designation of Chile as the next country with which to negotiate a trade agreement. Without Fast Track, it was unrealistic to believe that meaningful negotiations could move forward.

Recognizing this fact, the Clinton administration mounted another attempt to renew Fast Track in 1997 after the president's reelection. Even though Republicans continued to have a legislative majority, most supported trade agreements. So it was reasonable to expect that the president's proposal would pass. However, a group of conservative Republican representatives tied their support for Fast Track to dropping foreign aid to organizations that included abortion in their approaches to family planning.[47]

In addition, organized labor mounted a major campaign against renewal based on their fears that new trade agreements would mean a loss of jobs in the United States, a campaign endorsed by House minority whip and presidential aspirant Richard Gephardt and many of his Democratic Party colleagues. To avoid an embarrassing defeat in the House of Representatives, the Fast Track bill was never brought to a vote. Without Fast Track, any possibility that the Clinton administration could pursue the U.S. commitment to advance the FTAA by 2005 evaporated.

While some specialists believed that trade agreement negotiations could proceed even without Fast Track authority, the result for all intents and purposes was to scuttle prospects for the incorporation of other countries into new free trade agreements.[48] Chile in particular was affected, as it had been led to believe that it would soon be negotiating a free trade agreement that would place it in the same status with the United States as Mexico and Canada under NAFTA. Whether or not Fast Track renewal would have been sufficient in itself to move negotiations forward, the option was precluded by President Clinton's inability to overcome the divisions within his own party.

DECERTIFICATION OF COLOMBIA

Another example of Clinton administration decisions that produced an outcome creating a set of new challenges and problems for U.S. policy involved the decertification of Colombia in 1996 and 1997. Decertification is a controversial U.S. unilateral initiative under Congress's 1986 counter-drug legislation that requires the executive branch to certify annually the degree to which governments are cooperating in drug supply reduction efforts in producing and trafficking countries. Under the legislation, governments could be certified as cooperating fully, as not cooperating but with a waiver for considerations of national security, or as not cooperating and thus decertified. Any country that was decertified could lose all U.S. economic and military assistance except for humanitarian aid and counter-drug support.[49]

However, the annual certification process is not as straightforward as it might seem. Certification on drug cooperation is almost inevitably intertwined with other U.S. policy objectives in specific countries. Furthermore, decertification itself is a very blunt instrument when actually applied. Its use runs the risk of undermining bilateral relations in areas of concern deemed to be at least as important as cooperation on counter-drug policy.[50]

By the mid-1990s, concern over increased flows of cocaine, heroin, and marijuana from Latin America to the United States, in spite of significant U.S. counter-drug assistance, led to closer scrutiny of the region's governments and their levels of support for the programs. Latin American countries that are particularly important in assisting the U.S. effort to reduce illegal drugs production and supply include Mexico, Colombia, Peru, and Bolivia. Between them, they produce all the cocaine consumed in the United States, along with most of the heroin and about one-fifth of the marijuana.[51]

Although both Peru and Bolivia, the source of most coca leaf production in the mid-1990s, were deemed to be cooperating fully with U.S. efforts, Mexico and Colombia were seen as more problematic cases. Mexico, through which an estimated 70–80 percent of the illegal drugs were entering the United States at the time, had an untrustworthy and often corrupt police force and several examples of drug traffickers' influence over high officials with counter-drug responsibilities. Colombia, in turn, was the actual manufacturing source of most cocaine and heroin entering the United States.

Even though a strong case could be made that Mexican authorities posed a greater problem for carrying out effective counter-drug policies with the United States than their Colombian counterparts, the dense network of bilateral relationships with Mexico precluded serious consideration of decertification there.[52] With growing pressure on the administration from Congress and the American public to take a tougher line on drug issues, U.S. policy makers chose to focus on Colombia. In 1995, they decided that Colombian authorities were not cooperating well, and they decertified the country but gave a waiver out of national security considerations.

In the 1996 certification deliberations, however, U.S. officials received evidence indicating that the newly elected president, Liberal Party candidate Ernesto Samper, had accepted several million dollars from drug traffickers, assistance believed to have been decisive in his narrow runoff election victory. With the support of the U.S. ambassador to Colombia, Myles Frechette, who believed that a strong message needed to be sent to Colombians that democratic practice is corrupted when backed with drug money, the Department of State decertified Colombia in 1996 without a national security waiver.[53]

Among other measures, including the suspension of almost all economic assistance, President Samper's visa to travel to the United States was revoked. A year later, officials came to the same decision, even though there were indications that Colombia had been taking steps to improve cooperation on drug policy with the United States and in spite of Ambassador Frechette's conclusion that decertification this time would be counterproductive.[54]

Although other factors also contributed to the growing difficulties the Colombian government was confronting in trying to deal with its multiple internal problems, decertification eroded further the legitimacy of the country's elected officials and their ability to respond to the challenges they were facing. Both paramilitary and guerrilla forces increased significantly in size and operational capacity. Their access to resources generated by drug trafficking enabled them to become better equipped than the Colombian military and police, forcing the latter into defensive stances in much of the countryside. Political violence increased markedly, accelerating the declining ability of central government to mount an effective presence in large swaths of the country.

The growing precariousness of the situation in Colombia by the late 1990s led the Clinton administration to conclude that it needed to make a major commitment there to avert the growing possibility of state collapse. The response was Plan Colombia in 2000, a major infusion of military assistance with some support for strengthening democratic institutions as well.[55] Decertification certainly sent a strong message to the Colombian government on drug issues, but it also had the unintended consequence of contributing to a profound legitimacy crisis for the Colombian state itself that soon forced the U.S. government to mount a major rescue program.

DEMOCRACY VS. DRUGS IN PERU

As in Colombia, conflicting policy priorities toward Peru in the late 1990s sent a mixed message as to just what U.S. policy was trying to accomplish there. Democracy promotion was one major stated objective. After Peru's president Alberto Fujimori's 1992 *autogolpe*, the United States joined the OAS in taking strong steps to force its restoration in Peru within a year and a half, including the suspension of a major military training program. After Peru reestablished democracy in late 1993, resumed U.S. bilateral aid contributed to the strengthening of the Peruvian government and its ability to respond to an array of citizen needs in the aftermath of a major economic meltdown and generalized guerrilla warfare.[56]

The other major U.S. policy objective in Peru was to reduce the production and trafficking of illegal drugs. Along with financial support to reinforce democratic restoration there, during the same period the United States also substantially increased counter-drug assistance. The goal was to work with Peruvian counterparts to reduce coca leaf cultivation and cocaine paste transportation, mostly to Colombia, where it was refined into cocaine and sent on to the United States and Europe.

Over the next four years, U.S. support contributed to Peruvian police and military units' ability to eradicate coca plantings, provide resources for alternative agricultural development, and interdict small planes on their way to Colombia with cocaine paste. Prices for coca leaf plummeted, and areas under coca cultivation declined by over half. By the late 1990s, Peru ceased to be the world's largest producer of coca leaf.

Both components of U.S. policy appeared to be working in Peru. From the mid-1990s onward, however, the tension between promoting democracy and reducing drug supply grew markedly. After President Fujimori's reelection by a substantial margin in 1995, he and his administration progressively introduced measures that undermined the country's already fragile democracy. With a small but pliable congressional majority, they pushed through measures that significantly restricted free expression and democratic procedures. These included a blanket amnesty for human rights abuses by the military and police, arbitrary court appointments for supporters, bribes to newspaper owners to control the press, and intimidation of opposition figures.

Even so, U.S. officials continued to work closely with the Peruvian government on counter-drug activities. Their principal Peruvian collaborator on drug policy was Vladimiro Montesinos, head of the National Intelligence Service (SIN), the very individual who was simultaneously directing the covert campaign to keep Fujimori in power. Whatever qualms U.S. policy makers might have had about this other side of Montesinos were offset by his ability to deliver on the counter-drug policy and the successes in the field in reducing coca production and increasing interdiction of cocaine paste.

It was not until U.S. officials found evidence of official manipulation in the run-up to the 2000 presidential elections in which Fujimori was once again a candidate that they began to voice their concerns. They broke off their relationship with Montesinos and denounced his actions only upon learning that he was involved in arms trafficking to the Colombian guerrillas.

Montesinos and Fujimori fled the country, and the regime collapsed. In mid-November, a transition government of former opposition figures began the daunting task of bringing democracy back to Peru. U.S. officials, having backed Fujimori until almost the end, were largely relegated to watching the transition unfold from the sidelines.

Because of the positions taken by U.S. officials both before the political crisis and as it unfolded, they had little influence over the democratic transition process in Peru. Although supporting in principle both democratic practice and counter-drug commitments, U.S. policy as it played out in Peru favored drug supply reduction over democratic enhancement. By choosing to work through the architect of the country's dismantling of democracy because of what he appeared to be able to offer in attacking the drug problem, in this case U.S. policy makers tarnished their country's consistent commitment to democratic principles and practice, which had been in place since the end of the cold war.[57]

Chaos and Conundrums: President Clinton's Trips

A major advantage of high-level official trips abroad is that they help to focus government attention on policy issues relating to the country or countries and region being visited. In preparing for and following up on such travel, the multiple agencies of the bureaucracy involved with these countries have a major incentive to coordinate their concerns and work out differences. With fewer trips, there are fewer such opportunities, thus increasing the likelihood that the policies and strategies of individual agencies will lack coherence. Top official travel also gets the individuals involved to look more closely at the specific issues that are affecting relations with the governments of the countries visited and helps them develop personal relationships with their counterparts that can be utilized to help resolve problems.

It was no secret that President Clinton, most of his principal advisors, and his secretaries of state had little knowledge about or concern for Latin America. They also had many other serious international issues to deal with. Even so, it was unfortunate that the president did not travel to the region until his second term, a fact that his White House chief of staff and close personal advisor, Thomas "Mack" McLarty III, termed "a mistake."[58] Secretary of State Warren Christopher made only one brief trip to the region during his tenure, in February and March 1996. His successor, Madeleine Albright, was a more frequent visitor, with 11 short trips to 13 Latin American and Caribbean countries (several more than once); however, these accounted for just over 15 percent of the 72 official international trips she took while serving as secretary.[59]

President Clinton's brief trip to Mexico, Costa Rica, and Barbados in May 1997 was long on rhetoric but short on substance. A commitment to "build a better future" or to promise "no mass deportations of illegal immigrants to the Caribbean" hardly qualify as solid policy initiatives.[60]

His equally short visits to Venezuela, Argentina, and Brazil in October 1997 raised more issues than they resolved. The trip occurred just weeks after the United States lifted a 20-year ban on the sales of high performance aircraft, with an eye to selling Chile F-16 supersonic jet fighters.[61] In Venezuela, questions were asked as to whether that country's air force could secure similar planes, raising the specter of a new arms race in the region. In Argentina, Clinton's declaration that the government's commitment to international peacekeeping forces earned the country the special designation of "extra-NATO ally," but did not assuage official concerns over the implications of possible supersonic fighter plane sales to its neighbor, Chile. And Brazilian authorities were miffed by what appeared to be the new special status of its neighbor, Argentina, with the extra-NATO ally designation.[62] As a result, the visit was far from the unqualified success that had been anticipated.

When the president traveled to Santiago in April 1998 for the second SOA meeting, he talked of his administration's commitment to the FTAA. Without renewal of Fast Track, however, his counterparts concluded that he would be unable to match U.S. policy objectives with concrete progress. Even though other concerns were advanced during the meeting, particularly in support for education and for better follow-up mechanisms, there could be no progress on the matter of greatest concern for most of the region's governments at the time, greater trade integration.[63]

The irritations that surfaced on each of the president's trips reflected not only an apparent lack of prior agency coordination and solid background briefing but also an overall absence of a coherent U.S. policy strategy for Latin America. Initiatives suitable for the government of one country did not necessarily translate into an integrated approach to the region as a whole. On balance, these presidential visits symbolized a rather haphazard policy process with regard to Latin American issues, always troubling, but particularly so well into the second term of his administration.

Conclusions

These policy advances and challenges suggest the complexity of United States–Latin American relations during the Clinton years and the difficulty of building consistently on the policy momentum toward the region generated by both favorable international and regional circumstances and the multiple initiatives of its predecessor. The impression given, on balance, was of an administration that was unable to take full advantage of the opportunities provided, in spite of some successes, and that tended over time to lurch reactively from crisis to crisis instead of being able to maintain its earlier momentum.

The key question, of course, is why? What were the main forces and factors that kept the Clinton administration from being able to exploit the opportunities with which it was presented to build a coherent and consistent policy toward Latin America? These will be among the concerns addressed in chapter 4, which explores in greater detail several cases of U.S. policy initiatives and responses.

Latin American Policy during the Clinton Years

Case Studies of Success and Failure

The broad review of the Clinton administration's foreign policies in chapter 3 suggests a somewhat confounding combination of effective balancing of difficult choices in some instances with ill-considered responses in others. Clinton officials and the foreign policy bureaucracy were able to articulate an overall vision of U.S. priorities in the region rather early—in preparation for the 1994 Miami Summit of the Americas (SOA). This vision emerged through an extensive process of intra-agency interaction as well as consensus-building consultation with Latin American governments and nongovernmental actors. Over the course of the Clinton years, however, this general vision blurred in practice when faced with specific policy challenges or unexpected events.

The administration's approach to Latin American issues highlighted the difficulties of maintaining the coherence of an overarching vision of policy goals and objectives amid the need to forge specific responses to specific problems in the region. The decision-making process tended to be haphazard, even chaotic.[1] An additional difficulty arose from policy makers' calculations of what would satisfy domestic political constituencies that too often got in the way of policies based on more considered appraisals of national interest and longer-term objectives; "politics, after all, was the criterion on which [the Clinton] administration often made its choices and judged its results."[2]

As presented below, several more detailed cases of Clinton administration policy toward Latin America provide additional insights into difficulties encountered as well as elements that contributed to successful outcomes. Presented chronologically, they include the North American Free Trade Agreement (NAFTA) ratification, the failed *Harlan County* mission to Haiti, a blocked ambassadorial nomination, the first summit process and its aftermath, the resolution of the Peru-Ecuador boundary conflict, the circumstances leading to the signing of the Helms-Burton Act, and the conflicting policy priorities of promoting democracy and reducing drug production as played out in Peru.

These examples deal with only a sample of the full array of policies that could be highlighted. Nevertheless, they were selected in order to reflect the variety of challenges and complexities Clinton officials faced as they tried to deal with some of the difficult issues in the region, sometimes successfully, sometimes not. Once each case of success or failure is described and analyzed, the discussion that follows to conclude the chapter offers a summary discussion of what these cases suggest in the way of general insights about the policy process during the Clinton presidency.

Ratification of the North American Free Trade Agreement

The battle over NAFTA illustrates the challenges and complexities of securing congressional approval for a controversial piece of legislation. Success in this case demonstrates the importance of a firm commitment by the president and his willingness to get into the trenches and use every legal means at his disposal. Without such a personal involvement by Clinton, it is very likely that the NAFTA treaty would not have passed. Even so, it was a very close call and created other problems for the administration as a result.

Up until a few days before the decisive vote on November 17, 1993, it appeared that anti-NAFTA sentiment, concentrated within the Democratic Party and particularly among the party bastion of organized labor, could well prevail.[3] Treaty supporters groused that this was the case because the president had not started early enough to actively campaign for NAFTA, even though he had publicly reasserted his commitment to ratification in July. One illustration was that Clinton selected prominent Chicago lawyer Bill Daley as the head of the pro-NAFTA campaign in August but failed to give Daley a staff or an office before heading out on vacation.[4]

However, Clinton mounted a full court press that consumed most of his waking moments for several weeks. This included dozens of pro-NAFTA speeches across the country, scores of personal calls to wavering or undecided members of Congress, a dinner at the White House, and a virtual shuttle service to the White House from Capitol Hill for chats with both Democrats and Republicans.[5]

The president also vowed to crack down on Canadian wheat subsidies and limit citrus, sugar, and textile imports, thus winning over a dozen undecided representatives. A promise of more support for minority businesses garnered another key vote.[6] At the same time, Bill Daley was promising a variety of special projects and contracts to ensure support, commitments estimated to cost as much as $20 billion. When the House vote was taken, NAFTA prevailed, though by a scant 16 votes. A small number of "persuadable" Democrats gave Clinton a victory, even though most Democrats voted against the treaty (158 of 260).[7]

Clearly, Clinton's personal commitment to the ratification of NAFTA and involvement in the process, however belated, was decisive. However, other factors contributed to the ultimately successful outcome. One was the fact that Fast Track legislative authority was in place. This meant that only an up or down vote by Congress on the entire treaty was necessary. Another was that the previous Republican administration had already completed negotiations on NAFTA with Mexico and Canada by 1992. Furthermore, the three presidents had signed the treaties, and both the Mexican and the Canadian legislatures had ratified them. Not only did this set of developments put added pressure on the United States to go along, but it also predisposed most Republican members of Congress to support a treaty negotiated under the leadership of President George H. W. Bush.

In addition, the Clinton administration, fulfilling a campaign promise, negotiated side agreements on labor and environmental issues with Mexico and Canada before submitting NAFTA to Congress for a vote. This action served to mollify some wavering Democrats and gained their support even as others criticized the arrangements for not being strong enough.

The administration also mounted a major public relations campaign for NAFTA, enlisting scores of government officials to fan out across the country to speak on behalf of the treaty and bringing former presidents, Democrat Jimmy Carter and Republicans Jerry Ford and George H. W. Bush, to Washington to announce their support. Such efforts were reinforced by multimillion dollar lobbying that included both the Mexican government and major U.S. business interests.[8] A turning point in the public relations campaign, just days before the vote, was a highly publicized debate on primetime television between Vice President Al Gore and former presidential contender Ross Perot, a leading NAFTA critic. With Gore's decisive victory in the encounter, the momentum generated to that point by Perot's increasingly successful anti-NAFTA campaign was blunted virtually overnight.[9] The debate's outcome enabled the administration to take the initiative in what had been an uphill struggle.

By scheduling the decisive vote on NAFTA just days before a major meeting of U.S. and Asian heads of state on trade liberalization, Clinton put added pressure on legislators to demonstrate the U.S. commitment to the principles of free trade by passing the treaty. The larger context of ongoing General Agreement on Tariffs and Trade negotiations to set new trade standards as part of the Uruguay Round, in which the United States was a major participant, also favored ratification supporters.[10]

Without question, the passage of NAFTA represented a high point in Clinton's Latin American policy. Even so, victory exacted a high price. The political capital expended on ratification, as many of Clinton's advisors had feared, affected the president's ability to secure much of his domestic legislative agenda, from universal health care to deficit reduction. The political chits the president called in to secure support for NAFTA were then not available for other legislative priorities. The weeks of effort expended to pass the NAFTA treaty in a nonelection year left insufficient time for the administration to pursue politically sensitive proposals before Congress adjourned.

Furthermore, Clinton's commitment to NAFTA and his decisive role in securing its passage provoked deep alienation by organized labor, a key Democratic Party constituency. Labor's opposition kept many of its members on the sidelines during the 1994 midterm election campaign. The unwillingness of many labor locals to engage in their usual get-out-the-vote drives contributed to the Democrats' electoral defeat and loss of both houses of Congress in those elections. With Republicans in control of the legislative branch beginning in January 1995, a position they were able to retain for the rest of the decade, the president's ability to pursue his policy priorities on either the domestic or international fronts was severely tested.

Policy toward Haiti and the *Harlan County* Debacle

Bertrand Aristide, Haiti's first popularly elected president, was overthrown in a military coup in September 1991, the first in Latin America against an elected civilian government in 15 years. Between 1976 and 1991, the region had experienced a historically unprecedented generalization of electoral democracy and a consensus among the governments that democracy needed to be protected. Nevertheless, democratic restoration in Haiti proved elusive in spite of multilateral efforts under the recently agreed upon Organization of American States (OAS) Resolution 1080 to deal with just such a contingency.

The crackdown by the new military leaders against supporters of democracy in Haiti provoked the additional challenge of thousands of refugees from the island taking to small boats to seek safe haven, particularly in the United States. Although President Bush had committed the United States to restore Aristide to power, his administration faced the more immediate Haitian refugee problem. The U.S. government's response to what became a flood of over 30,000 Haitians was to round up as many as possible at sea and either return them or take them temporarily to the U.S. naval base at Guantánamo Bay.[11]

This was the scenario that faced Clinton when he took office in January 1993. In his election campaign he had promised to end Bush's approach to the Haitian refugee problem. However, after seeing evidence that up to 300,000 Haitians, anticipating a shift in U.S. policy, were preparing to flee, Clinton decided to keep the Bush policy in place but redouble efforts to restore democracy to Haiti.[12] He concluded that democratic restoration and the increased sense of political security it would bring was the only way to justify the return of refugees and to prevent new outflows.

However coherent and straightforward this goal appeared to be, in its pursuit the Clinton administration suffered a major setback in its Latin American policy. Why this occurred is related to the complex interaction of several factors that affected both policy formulation and implementation.

One important element was the high level of distrust between the principal Haitian actors themselves, Aristide and General Cedrás. Another was the often maddening and confounding approach President Aristide took in responding to proposals designed to work out solutions to each impasse and facilitate his return to Haiti; at times he would not respond at all, while at others he would initially agree, only to change his mind a few days later.

A third component involved significant differences in positions by different parts of the U.S. foreign policy bureaucracy. President Clinton and the National Security Council (NSC) were committed to Aristide and his restoration as Haiti's civilian head of state. However, the Central Intelligence Agency (CIA) had grave doubts about his mental stability and fitness for office, and the Department of Defense (DOD) was reluctant from the outset to use U.S. military forces in Haiti in support of the policy. Complicating the equation even further was the introduction of U.S. domestic political considerations. Groups of Aristide supporters in Washington, particularly the Congressional Black Caucus and TransAfrica, used the race card as well as his status as an elected head of government to continually pressure the administration to do whatever was necessary to put Aristide back in office as soon as possible.[13]

Against this complex backdrop, the administration decided to work through the United Nations to forge a workable solution. With Ambassador Lawrence Pezzullo, Department of State (DOS) special advisor to Haiti, as the U.S. representative, Ambassador Dante Caputo for the UN, and designated diplomats of the OAS and Friends of Haiti (Canada, France, Venezuela, and the United States), the parties were persuaded to meet on Governors Island in New York Harbor in July 1993 to work out an agreement for

Aristide's return. Not surprisingly, the negotiations were extremely difficult, and it was not certain until the very last minute that any agreement could be reached.[14]

Much of the uncertainty revolved around the maneuverings of Aristide, who would appear to support a solution at one moment only to backtrack almost immediately. At the eleventh hour, however, just as the Haitian military representatives were preparing to leave, he signed on. In exchange for the lifting of sanctions and a commitment to provide a multilateral force of police and military trainers and engineers who would carry only sidearms, General Cedrás agreed that Aristide could return to his former position by October 15.[15]

Preparations for the transition went forward at that point, with UN authorization in September for some 1,300 police trainers and monitors and military trainers and engineers.[16] Under this UN Mission in Haiti (UNMIH), a small advance party of military and police trainers arrived in Haiti by early October. In addition, about 250 civilian human rights monitors sponsored by the OAS/UN International Civilian Mission (ICM) spread out throughout the country.

From his Georgetown home, Aristide continued to express uncertainty over the arrangements and regularly undermined his principal ally in Haiti, Prime Minister Robert Malval.[17] Even though the situation in the country remained calm, according to both U.S. embassy accounts and the ICM human rights monitors, the UNMIH military trainer commander, U.S. Army colonel Gregg Pulley, was sending reports to DOD that alleged ongoing chaos and violence, none of which either the U.S. embassy or Ambassador Caputo saw.[18]

In the immediate aftermath of the Blackhawk Down tragedy in Somalia on October 3 and as the USS *Harlan County* was preparing to depart for Haiti with the multilateral contingent, however, a *New York Times* op-ed piece, apparently based on information leaked by DOD, deplored the deployment of U.S. forces to Haiti who would carry only sidearms. When Secretary of Defense Les Aspin went on a television talk show on October 10 to address the issue, a program broadcast in Haiti as well, he revealed that troops would also have boxes of M-16 rifles. Occurring just before the arrival of the *Harlan County*, this acknowledgment infuriated Cedrás, who concluded that the United States had deceived him with the promise that mission members would carry only light sidearms. At that critical moment, he ceased what had been a fluid communication with U.S. representatives in Haiti, setting the stage for the mission's failure.[19]

Vicki Huddleston, chargé d'affaires of the U.S. embassy in Haiti, had gone to the Port au Prince dock the morning of October 11 to receive the *Harlan County* when it arrived. However, she found the dock occupied by a Cuban ship and the port gates closed. Her efforts from her car at the entrance to the port to communicate with General Cedrás or the port director to resolve the situation proved fruitless. Soon afterward, a small mob of Haitians gathered around her convoy and staged what she saw as a highly orchestrated demonstration that threatened but did not actually carry out violence. At this juncture, she felt it prudent to leave the scene and return to the U.S. embassy.[20]

When the *Harlan County* steamed into the harbor a few hours later, it could not land and was soon surrounded by several small boats of demonstrators. Although Huddleston advised Washington that there were other docking options and that the *Harlan County* should remain until she had worked out arrangements, the ship's captain received orders to return to the United States, which he did the next day.[21] Both Haitians and all the officials who had worked so diligently to bring about the peaceful transition back to democracy were stunned. Their mission had failed, and the United States had been humiliated by the Clinton administration's decision to leave, taken without consultation with its representatives on the ground in Haiti.[22]

How can this action by U.S. policy makers in Washington, so inimical to U.S. interests and prestige, be explained? Certainly the chilling effect of the loss of U.S. Army Rangers' lives in Somalia weighed heavily in their decision. However, other factors were involved as well.

First, officials at DOD had never been comfortable with the mission. They became even less so with the negative reports from Haiti by Colonel Pulley, however wildly inaccurate. In addition, for reasons related to some of President Clinton's positions on military matters, they were not really sure that their chief executive had the military's best interests in mind. With grounds for doubt already established, DOD found a ready excuse to recommend aborting the mission in the aftermath of events in Somalia.

Second, Aristide's extended presence in Washington and his personal appeal led many there to be influenced by his repeatedly stated opposition to the Haitian military and his ambivalent stance on the negotiated solution at Governors Island. Furthermore, his constant maneuverings weakened Prime Minister Malval's ability to work through issues with the Haitian military leadership. At the same time, some high-level military and police officers, who continued to oppose Aristide's return under any circumstances, regularly undercut General Cedrás himself because they didn't think he was taking a tough enough line.[23]

Third, the CIA had regularly expressed its doubts about Aristide's mental stability and democratic instincts, which continued to resonate in some policy circles. In addition, the agency had an ongoing relationship with some of its less democratically inclined "assets" in Haiti that it was loathe to terminate. The result was to help strengthen the resolve of anti-Aristide forces, on the one hand, and to weaken the stated commitment of the Clinton administration to restore democracy, on the other.

In combination, these elements doomed the delicate process of working through a formula over several months for resolving Haiti's political morass. In the aftermath of its collapse with the withdrawal of the *Harlan County*, the country became more violent as antidemocratic elements organized and carried out assassinations and harassment of those who had worked for a peaceful solution. Although Clinton remained committed to restoring Aristide to office and his administration, with UN support, pursued harsh measures against the Cedrás regime, success did not come until just over a year later. Whatever the eventual outcome, the withdrawal of the *Harlan County* "was a disaster of the first magnitude, a personal one, and Clinton knew it."[24]

Death by Misadventure: The Failure of an Ambassadorial Nomination

Dr. Robert Pastor is a well-known figure in both foreign policy and academic circles. He served as director of Latin American and Caribbean Affairs on the NSC between 1977 and 1981 during the Carter administration.[25] Beginning in 1986, he taught political science at Emory University in Atlanta, and he became founding director of the Latin American and Caribbean Program at the Carter Center there. In these capacities, he wrote extensively on Latin American policy issues, participated in numerous election observer missions throughout the region, and advised Democratic presidential candidates, including Bill Clinton, on foreign policy.

Given Dr. Pastor's extensive experience and expertise on Latin American and Caribbean matters and his close identification with key figures of the Democratic Party, it was to be expected that he would serve in some important position in the Clinton administration. Since his NSC stint coincided with the historic negotiation and ratification of the Panama Canal treaties in 1978, in which he played an important role, Clinton's decision to nominate him as ambassador to Panama seemed appropriate.

But it didn't happen. Why a highly experienced and qualified individual did not become the U.S. ambassador to Panama offers insights on the complexities of the appointment process, the tensions between the executive and legislative branches, and the ability of a single powerful senator to thwart the will of the majority. The outcome also suggests how various elements could combine to produce results that most did not wish and that many worked diligently to avoid.[26]

Dr. Pastor was one of Bill Clinton's advisors on foreign policy issues during the presidential campaign, and most expected that he would enter the administration. A year passed, however, before he was informed that he would be nominated as ambassador to Panama. Then another six months passed before his papers went forward in June 1994 to the Senate Committee on Foreign Relations (SCFR).

Part of the delay can be explained by the tedious, redundant, and usually unnecessary vetting of the DOS security clearance, even though he already had a top secret clearance from the CIA. But the holdup also appears to have resulted from Pastor's close relationship with former president Jimmy Carter and the personal tension that existed between the former and current presidents.[27]

Even before the formal submission of the Pastor nomination, the SCFR's then ranking minority member, Jesse Helms, requested from Clinton on May 17, 1994, a raft of documents related to U.S. policy in Latin America between 1977 and 1981, that is, during the time that Pastor was serving on the NSC. Senator Helms's request focused on "all documents" relating to several sensitive areas.[28]

Three of the requests concerned U.S. policy toward Nicaragua. One was general in nature, and another related to President Carter's certification of September 1980 that the Sandinista government of Nicaragua was not supporting violence in other countries. The third request covered a much later period. It asked for all references to the Carter Center's (and Pastor's) role in the Nicaraguan elections and transition of 1990. A fourth request concerned any documents relating to gunrunning and narcotics trafficking activities by Panamanian leaders Omar Torrijos and Manuel Noriega between 1977 and 1981, which included the period during which negotiations over the Panama Canal treaties were completed and the treaties themselves were ratified. The fifth and final request concerned Grenada, specifically the ouster of Prime Minister Eric Gairy in 1979 by Maurice Bishop and his New Jewel Movement.

For the DOS Office of Congressional Affairs (H), which had formal responsibility for responding to Senator Helms's request, this was a daunting task indeed. By one estimate, complying fully would mean reviewing some 11.2 million pages, a task that would take 1,000 people working full time for five and a half years to complete, at a cost of $2.8 billion![29] By focusing primarily on DOS material, H identified thousands rather than millions of pages and delivered the first tranche of unclassified documents relating to the requests in late July and a second tranche of classified material in mid-August. Review of all this material was not completed by the SCFR until late September, more than two months after the committee's formal hearing on Pastor's nomination on July 22.[30]

The practical effect of the delay in receiving the documents requested was to postpone a final determination by the SCFR on the Pastor nomination until early October. Even though his nomination was overwhelmingly supported when it finally did come up for a vote on October 4, by a bipartisan 16–3 margin, Helms chose at that point to invoke the senatorial privilege of placing a hold on the nomination. This meant that the full Senate could not vote to confirm Pastor as ambassador to Panama, which appeared all but certain, before Congress recessed on October 8.[31]

With the Republican landslide victory in the November 1994 midterm elections, which gave the party a majority in both houses of Congress and brought Helms to the chair of the SFCR, any effort to reintroduce the nomination in the new Senate would be fraught with uncertainty. Accepting his fate, Pastor asked Clinton to withdraw his name from consideration, which he did.[32]

The objective appraisal of Dr. Robert Pastor's strong qualifications to become ambassador to Panama took a backseat to the objections of one powerful senator, who adroitly managed the mechanisms of the nomination process and the rules of the Senate to block his confirmation. Given the high level of support that the nominee enjoyed within the SCFR and the full Senate, it is possible that a favorable vote for confirmation could have been secured had Clinton sent the nomination forward earlier and had H been able to respond more quickly to the request for documents.

However, this case also points up the perils of prior high-level government experience, which on its face should be a point in favor of confirmation. Pastor's work on the NSC during a historic if controversial period in U.S. relations was held up to minute scrutiny. Senator Helms blamed him for pushing for President Carter's certification that the government of Nicaragua was not exporting violence to neighboring countries when some intelligence indicated it was. Helms also accused him of burying information about President Torrijos's gunrunning and drug trafficking to ensure passage of the Panama Canal treaties. And when, in his role as a Carter Center fellow, he was asked by Carter to advise and accompany him to Haiti in September 1994 to help facilitate a peaceful return to democracy there, where by all accounts he played an instrumental role in the successful outcome, he and the

DOS were excoriated for not clearing his participation in advance with the SCFR because he had already been nominated for the ambassadorship.[33]

None of these charges has much merit, but they highlight the challenges that face individuals who toil in the foreign policy arena to help bring about change in controversial areas when they are asked to return to government service in positions that require the advice and consent of the Senate. Such individuals, as the Pastor case demonstrates, are too likely to find themselves at the mercy of bureaucratic procedures, executive-legislative tensions, and an individual opponent in a key position whatever their actual qualifications for the posts for which they are nominated.

A Major Achievement, Qualified: The 1994 Summit of the Americas

The original idea for a meeting of all of the hemisphere's elected leaders emerged from various quarters in the immediate aftermath of NAFTA's ratification in November 1993. Proponents included some Latin American ambassadors in Washington, as well as some U.S. officials in DOS and the office of the USTR.[34] The NSC thought the moment propitious for an initiative to build on the momentum generated by NAFTA's passage and to take advantage of the "unprecedented convergence between the United States and Latin America on fundamental political and economic matters."[35] To this end, the NSC quickly drafted an action memorandum for Clinton's review and decision.

The memorandum proposed that the president invite Western Hemisphere heads of state to a summit meeting, the first since 1967.[36] With the enthusiastic support of Vice President Gore, Clinton approved the initiative. The decision-making process is unusual in this case because it was made rapidly and came from the highest levels of government rather than following the usual process of working its way up through official channels.[37] One reason this was possible was that the bureaucracy was already working on a comprehensive review of United States–Latin American policy that would eventually emerge as a Presidential Decision Directive (PDD) in September 1994.[38]

Since Gore was already going to Mexico to reaffirm U.S. commitment to NAFTA and to smooth ruffled feathers there after the bruising congressional ratification process, Clinton agreed that Gore would announce the SOA during his visit.[39] In his December 1, 1993, speech, the vice president extended an invitation to "the democratically elected presidents and heads of government of the Americas to a summit meeting to discuss ways of deepening hemispheric cooperation through economic integration and a shared commitment to democratic institutions."[40] Governments quickly announced their willingness to attend. They also pushed from the beginning for the inclusion of free trade area expansion as "the centerpiece of the summit agenda."[41]

The SOA initiative and the way it played out reflected a number of elements of the Clinton administration's Latin American policy process. The case illustrated the importance of publicly expressed support at the highest levels of government to increase the likelihood of success. It also demonstrated the benefits of close consultation on all aspects of the meeting with all parties involved, particularly among the participating countries. And it reflected how large and complex a task it is and how long it took to work through the layers of the U.S. foreign policy bureaucracy and the multiple domestic political considerations involved to forge agreement on specific issues, particularly those related to trade.

At the same time, the SOA process revealed the difficulties in securing effective follow-up with limited resources, incompletely constituted organizations, and a lack of presidential involvement. So however successful the SOA itself, the initiative highlighted many of the challenges involved in making effective policy.

Working out the details was a more complicated process than initially anticipated, and the actual SOA gathering itself could not be held until more than a year later, even though high-level U.S. government meetings on the topic began in February 1994 and Miami was announced as the meeting's venue in March. For the U.S. government, particularly within the USTR and the Department of the Treasury, the main issue was whether or not it was desirable to include consideration of the FTAA. These officials were concerned that such a proposal could complicate efforts to complete the Uruguay round of trade discussions through the General Agreement on Tariffs and Trade and the World Trade Organization. In addition, some of the president's political advisors worried that pursuit of an FTAA in the aftermath of divisions over NAFTA ratification could divide the Democratic Party even more by further alienating its labor constituency.[42]

These internal discussions delayed for several months a formal commitment by the U.S. government to the FTAA as part of the summit. President Clinton finally signed off on FTAA inclusion in October and made the formal public announcement in November, less than four weeks before the SOA was to take place. In addition, Clinton's assent for the inclusion of the specific date of 2005 for its completion, viewed as crucial by FTAA supporters within the administration and by Latin American governments, did not occur until just days before the meeting, and would have been unlikely without the pressure of the impending gathering.[43] According to one close observer, its somewhat chaotic and improvised nature was the result of the absence of a comprehensive strategic vision on trade.[44]

The other main reason for the delay, beyond the inevitable bureaucratic inertia when there are many months to prepare, was the extensive consultation process with hemisphere governments. High U.S. government officials, including Vice President Gore, Undersecretary of State for Economic, Business, and Agricultural Affairs Joan Spero, and Deputy Secretary of State Strobe Talbott, led six delegations between March and July to meet with officials of virtually all the countries in the region.

With the naming of Thomas F. "Mack" McLarty, President Clinton's close friend and advisor, as the White House coordinator for the SOA, Latin Americans were reassured that the project was supported at the highest levels of the U.S. government.[45] After the first draft of the SOA agenda prepared by U.S. government working groups was circulated to all hemisphere participants in August, a new round of multiple consultations took place between the parties and U.S. interagency working groups on good governance, women's rights, sustainable development, education, infrastructure, and microenterprise. Trade issue discussions took place as well, but much later and with a different structure in which the U.S. role was more dominant.[46]

Throughout the process, real consultation and accommodation to concerns highlighted the exchanges, which in many cases also included nongovernmental civil society actors. This permitted the final formulation and approval of a consensual SOA agenda at a meeting of vice ministers of all participating countries at Airlie House near Warrenton, Virginia, two weeks before the Miami gathering of the hemisphere's heads of state. The momentum generated by the "Spirit of Airlie House" consensus overcame any lingering doubts by participants that the United States was holding the SOA to pursue its own regional agenda and contributed to high expectations for important achievements at the meeting.

Without question, the SOA represented a high point in United States–Latin American relations during the Clinton years. The symbolic importance of bringing together 33 democratically elected heads of state and the normative significance of this unprecedented event cannot be underestimated. The inclusion of presidents-elect Ernesto Zedillo of Mexico and Fernando Henrique Cardoso of Brazil helped set the stage for greater cooperation with those governments.[47]

The extensive process of prior consultation with all the parties involved and with many nongovernmental organizations on specific issues helped to create the sense that the SOA was indeed a genuine collaborative enterprise of equals. Furthermore, the massive effort required within the U.S. government bureaucracy to translate a general proposal into a set of specific goals and initiatives indicated that the remarkably complex process of making U.S. foreign policy can produce results when participants perceive that top officials are committed to the enterprise.

The Declaration of Principles agreed upon—strengthening democracy, promoting prosperity through economic integration and free trade, eradicating poverty, and guaranteeing sustainable development—affirmed U.S. policy objectives as well as the aspirations of attendees.[48] In addition, the Plan of Action that accompanied these principles set out specific steps in 23 areas that participating states would take in collaboration as they worked to carry them out.[49] It was further agreed that there would be regular meetings in the future of the hemisphere's elected heads of state and that Chile would host the second summit in 1998.

For all of its accomplishments, however, the SOA also highlighted some of the challenges in the U.S. approach to inter-American relations. The problem of limited resources was one. Although new funding of $100 million was proposed for the SOA and its follow-up, the initiative was not vigorously pursued, so no new resources were appropriated.[50] This made it very difficult to provide the support necessary to ensure that mechanisms to implement the Plan of Action could be effective. The lack of resources also affected the choice of Miami, which was selected in large measure because key Democratic fund-raisers in that city agreed to find the money to pay for the meeting.[51]

The SOA follow-up mechanisms themselves presented another problem. U.S. policy makers decided that the Organization of American States would not be the appropriate institution to have responsibility for implementation.[52] However, the patchwork arrangements that were set up, which included a combination of various governments' agencies and nongovernmental entities to oversee the follow-up process, proved unwieldy. As a result, a number of the provisions failed to be implemented, and those that were depended on the individual initiative of individual governments and nongovernmental organizations.[53]

A third problem area related to President Clinton himself. Although he was the key decision maker for the SOA process, he was not involved in its details, so he lacked full engagement or commitment. In the SOA's aftermath, he was distracted by other issues and by the divisions within his own party over free trade expansion in the hemisphere. As a result, he was rarely engaged in follow-up after the meeting.[54]

Another difficulty developed over the extended debate within the U.S. government regarding the issue of the FTAA. Because agreement was achieved so late in the SOA preparation process, the mechanisms to pursue the U.S. commitment were never fully articulated. This lack complicated any satisfactory follow-up on trade integration, much to the consternation of the Latin American governments, who had worked diligently for U.S. support for free trade expansion as a core element of the summit. When the Clinton administration failed to secure renewal of Fast Track to facilitate new trade agreements in the hemisphere or legislation for access to NAFTA, their disquiet turned to disillusionment with the inability of the United States to make good on its promises.[55]

On balance, then, the Miami SOA, for all of its symbolic significance, failed to realize its promise in practice. Chile, which had every expectation of becoming the next Latin American entry to a free trade agreement with the United States, was left in the lurch. Even though inter-American trade expanded markedly during the 1990s even without additional formal agreements, many Latin American governments felt that they had been abandoned by the inability of the Clinton administration to make good on its commitment to establish the FTAA. The combination of internal U.S. government disagreement on the issue, internal Democratic Party division, Clinton's calculations based on domestic politics, and a recalcitrant Republican Party majority in Congress worked together to frustrate further progress in the hemisphere on free trade agreements.

Resolving an Intractable Conflict: The Ecuador-Peru Border Dispute

A nation's foreign policy is often subject to events over which it has no control but to which it must respond. During the Clinton years, several such unexpected developments occurred in Latin America that forced the administration to take action. Some, such as the Mexico peso crisis and the shoot-down of the Brothers to the Rescue planes by the Cuban air force, drew high-level attention from the administration and extensive coverage by the media.

Such responses stand in sharp contrast to those provoked by the unexpected outbreak of major armed conflict between Ecuador and Peru in January 1995 over what was at the time the longest running border dispute in the hemisphere.[56] After a brief initial flurry of media reporting and expressions of concern by U.S. officials, their focus soon turned to other matters. In spite of a general lack of high-level focus and follow-up concerning these hostilities, however, the ongoing beneath-the-radar involvement of U.S. actors over almost four years played a decisive role in eventually finding a definitive solution to the dispute.

The resolution of the Ecuador-Peru border conflict illustrates more than any other principle the crucial role of individual U.S. diplomatic leadership in slowly and patiently working through obstacles and resistances, challenges that, in this case, had developed on both sides of the frontier over almost two centuries. Other elements, nevertheless, also played a role in finding a way to solve the problem. One was the existence of a 1942 treaty between the two countries that included a multilateral mechanism of four "guarantor" countries, including the United States, to assist in helping the parties if requested. Another critical component was the willingness of the elected presidents of Ecuador and Peru to exercise leadership at a decisive juncture. Even so, as both governments asserted after the crisis had been overcome, no solution would have been possible without the deep and almost continuous involvement of the U.S. representative throughout the process.[57]

Ever since both countries had gained their independence in the first decades of the nineteenth century, they had tried and failed at least 13 times to resolve the boundary dispute through negotiated treaties or arbitration, had fought half a dozen wars without definitive results, and had engaged in close to 20 displays of force between 1950 and 1994.[58] After a brief 1941 war won decisively by Peru, the resulting 1942 treaty (Rio Protocol) appeared to set a definitive border. When geographic anomalies along the frontier showed up upon mapping in the late 1940s, however, Ecuador ceased participating with Peru in setting the final boundary demarcation as specified by the Rio Protocol and declared in 1960 that the treaty was null. Periodic skirmishes from the 1970s to the early 1990s, including a major confrontation in 1981, exacerbated tensions and set the stage for the 1995 outbreak.

As armed conflict enveloped the remaining disputed boundary area between January and March, Ecuador accepted once again the validity of the 1942 treaty and asked the guarantor states, Brazil, Argentina, Chile, and the United States, to assist in solving the dispute. The assistant secretary of state for inter-American affairs, Alexander Watson, quickly joined his counterparts from the other guarantors to work out some way to stop the fighting.[59] Meeting in Rio de Janeiro, they agreed to establish a small peacekeeping force of guarantor military in the disputed area to establish a cease-fire and then a demilitarized zone. Along with coordinated representations by guarantor diplomats, the peacekeeping initiative served as the incentive necessary for

Peru and Ecuador to cease military actions by March 1995 and within a few weeks to withdraw their forces from the disputed area. For the next year or so, the U.S. government agreed to provide the financial and logistical support needed to carry out this mission.[60]

While the initial objective of the guarantors was to stop the fighting, the longer-term goal was to find, if at all possible, some form of diplomatic resolution. Each guarantor was to select a representative to work toward this goal. Ambassador Watson concluded, in consultation with his colleagues, that the ideal U.S. diplomat for this task would be Ambassador Luigi Einaudi, a respected Latin American specialist with over two decades of service in policy planning positions in the Department of State as well as a stint as the U.S. ambassador to the OAS between 1989 and 1993.[61]

Ambassador Einaudi accepted the assignment and soon began to work with the other guarantor representatives on the problem. All were distinguished and respected professionals, and all except Einaudi had continuing responsibilities in their own foreign ministries that limited the time they could devote to the Peru-Ecuador crisis. Partly for this reason, they selected Einaudi as the guarantor intermediary to represent the body between formal meetings; this made him, in effect, the first among official equals. In this role, he came to be trusted by all for his judgment, his fairness, his discretion, and his scrupulous adherence to appropriate procedures. Following the central principle that the parties themselves must lead, he slowly and painstakingly guided the process to a successful conclusion.[62]

Various unexpected challenges along the way delayed and almost derailed the negotiations, however. One was the reluctance of U.S. officials, still wary of peacekeeping missions after Somalia, to continue their financial and logistical support for the guarantor military mission after the first year. Fortunately, Brazil stepped in to assume the crucial logistical role, and both Ecuador and Peru agreed to fund most of the mission's expenses. Other problems included major internal crises in both Ecuador and Peru in early 1997, Ambassador Einaudi's illness and retirement from the DOS, and presidential elections in Ecuador in 1998.

At the explicit request of both Ecuador and Peru, Einaudi was persuaded to continue in his post as the U.S. guarantor representative. Nevertheless, even after securing agreement on most remaining issues between the two parties by separating them into discrete negotiations, he and his guarantor colleagues could not get the two presidents to determine the final boundary settlement due to the deep and long-standing political sensitivities involved on each side. Given this impasse, the guarantors were able to persuade Jamil Mahuad, the newly elected president of Ecuador, and Alberto Fujimori of

Peru to ask their legislatures to allow the guarantors to determine the definitive settlement, which both did.

The basic problem was that Ecuador could not accept any resolution that did not provide some territorial concession, and Peru could not accept any resolution that did. With the concurrence of the guarantors and prior agreement by the two presidents, Einaudi devised a solution that gave Ecuador access to one square kilometer of territory in the area of the fiercest fighting, on the Peruvian side of the border, but as private property, and gave Peru the border demarcation originally laid out in the Rio Protocol. Once the congresses had agreed to allow the guarantors what amounted to binding arbitration, the solution was made public and both countries signed the final document on October 26, 1998. The longest enduring and in many ways the most intractable border dispute in the hemisphere had finally been resolved.[63]

The diplomatic process of resolving border problems took place with little public fanfare in the United States and without more than occasional involvement by top U.S. officials. This success demonstrated the degree to which the exercise of U.S. diplomatic leadership by a single individual with the authority and the room to work for whatever time was needed could contribute to an outcome that reflected well on the United States and benefited all the parties involved, even when working within the constraints of extremely limited resources and official indifference at the upper levels of the bureaucracy.

"Reports of My Death Have Been Greatly Exaggerated:" Cuba and the Helms-Burton Act

Relations with Cuba have posed multiple challenges for every U.S. president since Dwight D. Eisenhower. Since the 1962 agreement with the USSR in which Soviet missiles were removed from the island in exchange for a U.S. pledge not to invade Cuba with military force, U.S. policy makers have had to find other ways to accomplish their objective of removing Fidel Castro from power. Nothing has succeeded—neither the "stick" of the economic embargo nor the "carrot" of facilitating contacts with the island, negotiating diplomatic normalization, fostering cultural exchanges, or expanding Cuban exile visits. Over time, the million-strong Cuban American community, concentrated in Florida, has become an important actor in U.S. domestic politics. As a result, U.S. policy toward Cuba is often subject more to its effect on gaining Cuban American votes than on objective considerations of national interest.

The 1992 Cuba Democracy Act (CDA) was sponsored by Representative Robert Torricelli (D-NJ). Its formulation involved close consultation with the Cuban American National Foundation (CANF), a formidable lobbying group led by Jorge Mas Canosa that was established in the early 1980s to pursue U.S. government support of restrictive policies toward Cuba. The CDA proposed the closing of loopholes in the embargo by prohibiting U.S. subsidiaries abroad from trading with Cuba and ships that unloaded cargo in Cuba from docking in a U.S. port for six months. At the same time, it relaxed restrictions on travel to the island from the United States by Cuban Americans.

President George H. W. Bush initially opposed the bill, but candidate Clinton embraced it as a way to wrest Cuban American financial and electoral support from Bush in Florida. Outflanked on the right by his challenger, Bush responded by belatedly supporting the bill and signing it into law just two weeks before the 1992 election. Although Clinton was unsuccessful in bringing Florida into the Democratic column, he did gain about 20 percent of the Cuban American vote, a significant increase over Michael Dukakis's 5 percent in 1988.[64]

Once elected, Clinton continued his public support for the CDA and the embargo on Cuba in a clear effort to appeal to CANF and the Cuban American community even as most of his advisors advocated a relaxation of restrictions. Over the summer of 1994, however, the growing problem of Cuban immigration in the context of widespread U.S. domestic concern over immigration issues provoked a reassessment by administration advisors of the long-standing policy of granting Cuban refugees virtually automatic U.S. residency. Although not involved in the discussion, Clinton agreed to a policy shift and supported the transfer to Guantánamo Bay of Cubans intercepted at sea.

In the face of immediate expressions of outrage by CANF and the Cuban American community, however, the president hastily met with Mas Canosa and others and mollified them by invoking new sanctions on Cuba. These included expanded broadcasting by Radio and TV Martí and restrictions on travel and remittances to the island. Over the next several months, Clinton administration officials worked out agreements with the Castro government, finalized in May 1995, to provide up to 20,000 visas a year for Cuban emigration to the United States in exchange for stopping illegal emigration and acceptance of the return of Cubans intercepted at sea or already at Guantánamo Bay.[65]

Clinton's responses to both the immigration problem and CANF pressures reflected his calculations of their impact on domestic politics rather than foreign policy considerations. They also suggest the rather haphazard and ad hoc nature of the decision-making process in the Clinton White House.[66]

After Republicans took control of both houses of Congress in January 1995 following their sweeping midterm election victory, Cuba was one of many items on the new congressional leadership's legislative agenda. Jesse Helms became chairman of the Senate Foreign Relations Committee and set out immediately to put his stamp on U.S. policy toward the Castro government. He was particularly concerned about some reports suggesting that President Clinton might use his authority to normalize relations with Cuba, an initiative to which he was utterly opposed.[67]

With Helms staff assistant Dan Fisk coordinating the initiative, a draft bill was crafted that would require a democratic transformation in Cuba as an explicit condition for any U.S. normalization of relations. Under its provisions, the long-standing embargo was to be tightened and expanded to include the right of U.S. citizens to sue foreign companies that had taken over their former properties confiscated by the Castro government. In addition, executives and family members of such offending foreign companies would be denied visas to enter the United States. The bill also contained provisions to codify the embargo into law. This would have the effect of removing the embargo from executive control for the first time and placing it in the hands of the legislative branch.[68]

The bill, first presented by Senator Helms in February, not surprisingly met with strong Clinton administration opposition. Officials argued that the existing Cuba Democracy Act of 1992, with its two-track approach of sanctions and inducements as determined by the executive, was sufficient. Although the House passed the bill by a large majority (294–130) in September, it appeared that an administration counteroffensive against the legislation, one that included significant corporate backing, would be sufficient to prevent a favorable vote in the Senate. While the president never explicitly threatened a veto if the bill passed, Secretary of State Warren Christopher had indicated in correspondence with Congress that he would advise Clinton to exercise his veto power. Over the succeeding weeks, the administration's strategy of finding a way to avoid a Senate vote altogether seemed to be working.[69]

The February 24, 1996, Cuban air force shoot-down of the Brothers to the Rescue planes over international waters, completely changed the political dynamics of Helms-Burton. As Richard Nuccio, the president's special advisor on Cuba at the time, noted, Castro had "created a veto-proof majority" for the bill.[70] Clinton immediately condemned Cuba's action and supported new negotiations with Congress to draft and pass Helms-Burton.

With Congress now in the driver's seat, Senate negotiators were able to insist in meetings with administration representatives that the embargo be codified into law as part of the bill. They also reinserted the provision granting authority to deny visas to corporate executives of foreign companies holding former U.S. citizens' property in Cuba, and insisted that the president not be allowed the right to waive this article. Senate representatives did agree, however, to give the president authority to waive the implementation of provisions allowing suits against foreign companies (mostly Spanish, English, and Canadian) in possession of such properties.[71]

On these terms, the revised Helms-Burton bill passed both houses, and Clinton signed the bill into law on March 12, 1996. Although Latin American policy specialists in the administration opposed the president's decision, his political advisors argued that he really had no choice in the matter.[72]

On its face, Helms-Burton signaled a major setback for those in the Clinton administration who had supported initiatives to progressively open up channels for dialogue and cooperation. Nevertheless, Clinton did his best to pursue as open a policy toward Cuba as possible within the constraints imposed by Helms-Burton. He repeatedly waived implementation of the provision allowing suits against foreign companies. In the context of the pope's visit to Cuba early in 1998, he relaxed restrictions on travel and remittances and resumed cooperation on drug and immigration issues as well.[73]

Even so, the Cuban Liberty and Democratic Solidarity Act represented the reassertion of congressional prerogatives over executive authority and limited the ability of President Clinton or his successors to pursue a more independent course on relations with Cuba without securing legislative consent. The ongoing saga of U.S. policy toward Cuba during the Clinton years also points up the degree to which this president, like his predecessors, approached the issue based more on calculations of domestic political impact than on U.S. national interest considerations. Clinton reinforced the observation, attributed to Wayne Smith, former Foreign Service officer and chief of the U.S. Interest Section in Cuba, that U.S. policy toward Cuba is made not in Washington but in Miami.

Drugs or Democracy? The Tension between Policy Objectives in Peru

The Clinton administration, following both the lead of its predecessor and its own convictions, supported without hesitation the maintenance and deepening of the democratic procedures and practices that had been re-established in Latin America during the 1980s. At the same time, officials continued to pursue the counter-drug policies formulated in Congress and implemented in the region over several administrations.

The case of Peru posed special challenges on both policy fronts for U.S. policy as Clinton took office. Democracy in Peru was under siege from a major insurgency, a profound economic crisis, and the government itself; in 1992, the elected president, Alberto Fujimori, had suspended constitutional procedures in an *autogolpe* (self-coup). As the world's leading coca leaf producer with an expanding annual output, Peru also posed a serious drug supply problem for the United States.[74]

As U.S. policy toward Peru played out, support for democracy was tempered by the administration's efforts to reduce drug production and trafficking there. A combination of factors contributed to a policy that progressively favored counter-drug initiatives over insistence that Peru's government retain both the forms and the substance of democratic procedure and practice.

Within the U.S. policy-making process, key elements affecting it included congressional insistence that the Clinton administration pay more attention to the drug problem. Another was a strong drug czar in the White House after 1996 who was able to garner new resources and to push the bureaucracy on the problem—often at the expense of other policy priorities. A third involved the U.S. intelligence community, which was anxious to retain a key contact in Peru.

Within Peru itself, the government's leadership, which enjoyed public approval levels of 50–80 percent for most of its 11 years in power, was able to exploit for its own purposes the higher priority of U.S. policy makers to reduce drug production. Offering full cooperation on U.S. counter-drug policy helped Peru's leaders deflect attention from their progressive perversion of democratic procedures, beginning in 1995, in order to hold on to political power beyond their constitutionally mandated two terms. When largely internal pressures forced an unexpected, rapid, and dramatic collapse of the Fujimori regime's authoritarian project in late 2000, the limitations of U.S. policy became apparent.

At its outset, however, the Clinton administration had supported the OAS in its efforts under the 1991 Santiago Resolution (Resolution 1080) to restore democracy promptly in Peru. With a new constitution and congressional elections in late 1993, the country's resumption of democracy triggered the restoration of International Financial Institution (IFI) and U.S. bilateral economic support. Renewed democracy also justified expanded direct U.S. counter-drug assistance within the ongoing Andean Initiative, as well as Peru's belated inclusion into the 1991 Andean Trade Preference Act. The main purpose of this act was to foster more legal exports to the United States from the major drug-producing countries through tariff reductions for over 700 products.

By 1994, democracy and economic growth had resumed, inflation had been tamed, and the insurgency had been largely subdued. Peru, with substantial U.S. help and encouragement, finally appeared to have overcome its profound economic and political crises.[75]

However, after President Fujimori's reelection in 1995 in a process OAS observers deemed both free and fair, disquieting signs gradually emerged of the manipulation of democratic procedures to ensure the government's continuity in office. One disturbing measure was a general amnesty for the military for human rights abuses. Another involved the dismissal of Constitutional Tribunal members who opposed a third successive term for the president. The Fujimori government also prevented a popular referendum on a third term, even though its supporters had complied with all of the constitutional requirements. A further example was a steady campaign by the government to place most independent media outlets in the hands of administration sycophants. The architect of these moves to ensure political continuity was Fujimori's closest advisor and director of the National Intelligence Service (SIN), Vladimiro Montesinos, who also had responsibility for Peru's counter-drug strategy.[76]

U.S. policy makers saw Montesinos as an important intelligence asset—indeed, he had been on the CIA payroll for years—and he could be counted on to get things done on the drug front.[77] They came to rely on him for information and support that was unavailable from other sources in Peru. Both the U.S. drug czar, General Barry McCaffrey, and the ambassador to Peru, John Hamilton, continued to work with Montesinos long after clear indications had emerged of his involvement in undermining democratic procedures to help maintain the Fujimori government in power.[78] Only after evidence emerged in mid-2000 that Montesinos had directed a gunrunning scheme with several high Peruvian military officers to supply Colombian guerrillas with arms ostensibly purchased for the Peruvian army did the United States formally break its long-standing relationship with the SIN director.[79]

One of the difficulties U.S. policy makers had faced in the mid-1990s in their relations with Peru was access to Fujimori and other top figures in his government. Between 1993 and 1999, neither U.S. ambassador Alvin Adams nor his successor, Dennis Jett, was ever able to meet with Fujimori beyond ceremonial occasions, an ongoing situation that served to increase the importance of the U.S. relationship with Montesinos. In the case of Ambassador Jett, at least, the explanation can be attributed to his outspokenness regarding the actions of the Peruvian government that were weakening democracy.[80]

When Ambassador Hamilton arrived in late 1999, however, he made an effort, under instructions from Washington, to reopen lines of communication with Fujimori and others, and he succeeded. In his view, he could accomplish more by quiet persuasion than by public scolding, and over the course of his tenure as ambassador he believed that he had made the U.S. position supporting democracy clear to key figures in the Peruvian government.[81] Certainly government-to-government relations improved through Hamilton's initiatives. However, such improvement occurred in a local context of growing indications that democratic procedures were being hijacked by the Fujimori administration to ensure victory in the April 2000 elections.

It was not until late January 2000, after institutional mechanisms were in place to bring about a favorable electoral outcome, that Hamilton articulated publicly the U.S. government's concern about the quality of democracy in Peru.[82] And only in the aftermath of the April election itself, when it was becoming clear that the Peruvian government was manipulating the count to ensure a first-round victory (at least 50 percent of the valid vote), did the U.S. government weigh in with its big guns, including President Clinton and Secretary of State Madeleine Albright, to protest what was happening. Their statements, along with those of virtually the entire international community, were thought to have kept Fujimori from declaring victory on the first ballot.[83]

Nevertheless, Fujimori went on to win the second round after the second-place candidate, Alejandro Toledo, withdrew from the race in protest. In the midst of growing opposition among Peruvians and large-scale demonstrations, Fujimori was inaugurated in July for his blatantly unconstitutional third term.

Within four months, however, the Fujimori era was over. The spark was the airing of a videotape on Peru's one remaining independent television station in September that showed Vladimiro Montesinos bribing an opposition congressman to join the Fujimori forces. In spite of the Peruvian president's efforts to stem popular outrage by distancing himself from his close advisor and by calling new elections the next year in which he would not be a candidate, he was unable to remain in power.[84]

Fearing the political chaos that could ensue were Fujimori not to remain at the helm for the transition, U.S. officials worked through Ambassador Hamilton to facilitate Montesinos's exile to Panama and to persuade Fujimori to remain in office until the new elections. However, the president fled to Japan in mid-November; the Peruvian congress, now in opposition hands, declared his office vacant; and a transition government took control. Slowly but surely, democracy was restored to Peru. The efforts of the Peruvians themselves, however, rather than outside actors, explain the success of the political transition back to democracy.[85]

Although concerned about both democracy and drugs in Peru, the Clinton administration devoted most of its attention to the drug issue. U.S. officials continued to work with an individual who could and did help them to make significant progress on reducing coca production and cocaine paste trafficking, even though this same person was the architect of multiple initiatives to weaken democratic practices and procedures. Whether a more forceful U.S. approach to oppose the antidemocratic measures pursued by the Fujimori regime would have been sufficient in itself to prevent Peru's decline into authoritarianism is not clear. However, it certainly is the case that the greater focus on counter-drug policy contributed to democracy's crisis there by the degree to which it relied on an utterly unscrupulous individual. Furthermore, as the crisis unfolded, U.S. preoccupation with the potential for political chaos contributed to the decision to continue to support President Fujimori, bringing even greater discredit to the ostensible U.S. commitment to democratic procedures and practices.

Conclusions

The seven cases of U.S. policies relating to Latin America during the Clinton years discussed above offer more detailed descriptions of context, concerns, and outcomes in these specific arenas of the pursuit of U.S. goals and interests. They also highlight a number of important factors that influenced the policy process over the eight years of the administration and that bore significantly, even decisively at times, on its outcome.

One is the degree to which the president exercises leadership and per-sonal involvement in the process. Under most circumstances, the more fully and publicly engaged the chief executive is with a particular policy, the more likely a positive outcome. In pursuing NAFTA through to suc-cessful ratification, for example, Clinton's commitment manifested itself in virtually full-time dedication to mobilizing support through scores of phone calls, meetings, and speeches. True, he started late and paid a high political price among his core supporters within organized labor. Nevertheless, there is general agreement that his willingness to take the time necessary to do whatever had to be done to marshal the necessary votes for passage was a decisive element in gaining final approval.

The president's early and unwavering support for the SOA helped galva-nize the U.S. government bureaucracy into action to put together a compre-hensive policy approach. His desire to ensure a successful outcome as the meeting days neared pushed those U.S. policy makers who were dragging their heels on the trade issue to agree to the inclusion of the FTAA on the agenda and to set a specific date for the completion of negotiations. The suc-cess of the Miami SOA meeting itself, then, owes much to Clinton's ongo-ing and publicly expressed commitment. In policy areas where presidential leadership was limited or lacking, as in following up on the implementation of the various commitments of this first summit's ambitious Plan of Action, particularly with the FTAA, success was limited or not achieved at all.

A second factor suggested by the cases is the importance for specific policy outcomes of the role played by individuals below the highest levels of leader-ship. When a particular issue or world region lies outside a central concern of top officials, as matters relating to Latin America often do, the quality and capacity of middle-level leadership assumes greater importance.[86] Nei-ther President Clinton nor his secretaries of state had any particular interest or experience in hemispheric affairs and had many other pressing crises in other parts of the world to deal with. By many accounts, however, either through a lack of confidence in their abilities, their own policy management style, or both, they tended not to give DOS officials at the assistant secretary level the authority or the space they needed to carry out policy in their areas of expertise.[87]

The result, in addition to less coherence and effectiveness in dealing with specific issues, was that DOS was often unable to serve as a strong counter-weight within the foreign policy bureaucracy to other actors with concerns about particular issues in the region. This enabled DOD, White House advi-sors, Congress, and other agencies to weigh in to affect policy outcomes.

Examples include the application of the Governors Island Accord in Haiti, the Helms-Burton legislation on Cuba, and the emphasis on counter-drug policy over democracy in Peru.

Even within such constraints, however, individuals did have a major impact on the policy process and its outcome. One such example is Ambassador Einaudi's role over more than three years in helping to work through a particularly difficult border dispute between Ecuador and Peru.

General Barry McCaffrey, in his position as director of the White House Office on Drug Control Policy, is another. He played a major role in Latin American policy during his tenure through the exercise of strong leadership on drug-related issues. This is demonstrated, among other initiatives, by his ability to gain the support of both DOD and Congress for new resources to fight the drug problem, even as appropriations for other foreign policy agencies were declining.[88] While one result of his effectiveness was a disproportionate focus on counter-drug policies in Latin America at the expense of other priorities, as the Peru case illustrates, he also demonstrated the impact a single person in a midlevel role can have on the process.

A different kind of example of the exercise of leadership was that of Senator Helms, with his ability, almost single-handedly, to block the ambassadorial appointment of Robert Pastor through delaying tactics and the use of senatorial privilege. On the other hand, the experience of Ambassador Pezzullo as the secretary of state's special advisor to Haiti pointed up the limitations of individual leadership in a critical situation. It proved impossible for him to overcome the myriad personal, institutional, situational, and procedural resistances that combined to cause the failure of the Governors Island Accord implementation, in spite of the extraordinary energy, personal capacity, and wealth of experience he brought to the task.

A third policy consideration illustrated by the case studies is the effort required to bring a complex and often internally competing bureaucracy to focus on a specific issue and to work through the political underbrush to put together a coherent and effective proposal. The SOA preparation experience demonstrated both the time required for the task and the fact that it could be done, and done well, in almost every area of concern.

However, this complex policy-making process also highlighted how serious disagreement, in this case on the trade issue, could delay resolution to a degree that contributed to an inability by the United States to follow up effectively on what was the top priority of most Latin American governments at the time of the SOA meeting. The difficulty of marshaling the U.S. government bureaucracy to coordinate and commit to a specific foreign policy initiative, at least toward Latin America, was illustrated by the fact that the

Miami SOA preparations turned out to be the only time during the Clinton administration that such coordination happened to this degree.

A number of the cases also highlight a fourth policy consideration—the impact of domestic politics on foreign policy. While this is a fact of political life that affects foreign affairs in any U.S. administration, domestic political considerations tended to weigh more heavily on foreign policy during the Clinton years. This was due in large part to President Clinton's greater interest in and experience with state and national politics and to his finely tuned political instincts.

The negotiation of labor and environmental side agreements as part of NAFTA reflected the president's sensitivity to domestic politics. While instrumental in winning ratification, they were not perceived as strong enough to satisfy important Democratic Party constituencies. Contrary to President Clinton's hopes, labor's disillusionment over NAFTA, even with the side agreements, was an important factor in the Republican Party gains in the 1994 midterm elections, with serious negative consequences for the administration's subsequent ability to pursue its policy agenda.

Policy toward Haiti was very much affected by Clinton's concern over the political effects of immigration as well as by the Congressional Black Caucus's pressure to restore President Aristide to power in spite of the doubts expressed by some government agencies about his democratic credentials. Haiti policy was also complicated by Clinton's difficult relationship with the U.S. military establishment and, as a result, the need he felt, in addition to his own personal qualms, to give greater weight to DOD concerns over the deployment of U.S. troops to that troubled nation.

Significant differences between the president's political advisors and Latin American specialists within the NSC and the White House often affected policy decisions, such as with Haiti and the USS *Harlan County* and with Cuba and the Helms-Burton legislation. However, it may also be argued in both cases that unexpected external events had a major impact as well and contributed to decisions that did not advance U.S. foreign policy goals in either.

The Republican Party's dramatic midterm election victory in 1994, which gave it control of both houses of Congress for the first time since the 1950s, occurred in spite of the president's hope that delaying renewal of Fast Track would produce a better political outcome. The subsequent reassertion of congressional prerogatives in foreign policy forced the administration to consider legislators' concerns and to try to assuage them. One example was to respond to congressional demands to reemphasize counter-drug policies; another was to recognize that the Pastor ambassadorial nomination could not go forward and to ask that Dr. Pastor withdraw his name from consideration.

A fifth factor that can be derived from the cases is the degree to which foreign policy was reactive rather than proactive. Events often forced or precipitated decisions, as illustrated by the effects on Haitian policy of U.S. military deaths in Somalia, the shift in Cuban policy due to the shoot-down of the Brothers to the Rescue planes, and the need to respond to the outbreak of hostilities between Ecuador and Peru.

When the events generated greater publicity and had a larger impact on public opinion, as with Somalia and the Brothers to the Rescue, the administration's immediate policy responses were less effective in accomplishing previously stated objectives. Where the effect on public opinion was less, as in the border conflict, U.S. officials were able to work largely unnoticed to find an appropriate and lasting solution that benefited all parties.

The success of the Miami SOA, with its articulation of an overall set of policy objectives in Latin America, however general, laid the foundation for what could have been significant policy advances in the region. However, the Mexican peso crisis that followed almost immediately redirected both public and bureaucratic attention. By the time the dust had settled and the problem had been dealt with effectively, the opportunity to build on the summit success had slipped away.

A final factor suggested by some of the cases, as well as by the more general discussion of Clinton administration policy toward Latin America in chapter 3, is the degree to which the foreign policy process takes place largely out of public view. The extensive interaction within the bureaucracy and with Latin American counterparts that was required to formulate the Miami SOA document is one example. Another was the significant and ongoing behind-the-scenes involvement of U.S. officials that helped to bring the parties together in Guatemala to find a peaceful resolution to the long-standing guerrilla war there under UN auspices. A similar quiet but continuing process of working with Mexican authorities and political actors to encourage a more open democratic process contributed to the most transparent elections in that country's history in 2000. The eventual success in helping to resolve the most difficult and deep-seated border dispute between Peru and Ecuador represented another triumph of quiet diplomacy.

While the cases presented above reflect only a sample of the policy concerns of the Clinton administration, they serve to highlight the variety of factors that influence the foreign policy process in its efforts to deal effectively and appropriately with issues that affect Latin America. They indicate the major considerations that bear on policy and the elements that contribute to eventual success or failure. On balance, they suggest the degree to which Latin American policy during the Clinton years was unable to take full advantage of the favorable context of the early 1990s and lost a historic opportunity in a number of areas to advance U.S. priorities in the region and to respond to some of the major concerns of the hemisphere's governments.

The chapter that follows provides an overall assessment of the Latin American policies of the Clinton administration by focusing on a different set of indicators—namely, its stated policy objectives. To what degree was the administration able to achieve its major goals in the region—enhancing democracy, achieving economic growth through free trade, reducing poverty, and securing sustainable development?

Latin American Policy during the Clinton Years

An Assessment

This chapter brings together the strands of the analysis in the body of the volume to provide an overall summary characterization of the Clinton administration's Latin American policy. The administration did articulate a set of policy objectives toward the region and was able at times to make difficult decisions and see them through to successful outcomes. On the other hand, the pursuit of specific policies was all too often affected in negative ways by the variety of forces, pressures, and events discussed in chapters 3 and 4. While such limiting factors are inherent to the U.S. policy process, they seemed to weigh more heavily on more occasions during the Clinton years. To a greater extent than on George H. W. Bush's watch, one combination or another produced results in various policy arenas that did not advance U.S. interests in Latin America.

The overall assessment of President Clinton's Latin American policies is based primarily on an analysis of his administration's four principal objectives in the region, laid out at the first Summit of the Americas (SOA) in Miami in December 1994. The chapter begins by stating them and briefly characterizing the progress or lack of progress made for each. Then the chapter analyzes in greater detail the degree to which each stated objective advanced over the 1990s through sets of longitudinal data that provide measures of various aspects of the four policy goals. Finally, a concluding discussion encapsulates the analysis with a summary of why the Clinton administration failed to accomplish its overarching policy goals in the region in spite of some positive outcomes in several discrete policy areas.

Policy Objectives: A Summary Evaluation

1. Preserving and strengthening democracy. Democratic forms were generally retained, but many governments became increasingly racked by crises of corruption, increased criminal activity, political violence, and restrictions on democratic practice. Drug production increased, with its attendant violence and corruption. Popular confidence in democracy declined.

2. Promoting prosperity through economic integration and free trade. Over the course of the Clinton years, there were significant advances in the region in economic liberalization, foreign investment, and increased trade. These combined to produce modest net economic growth in Latin America for the decade, in spite of a recession between 1997 and 2000. However, the failure to expand the free trade area or to incorporate additional countries into NAFTA-type agreements meant that most of the effects of these advances were concentrated in Mexico. In addition, there was a lack of significant new job creation in Latin America; high unemployment and underemployment continued to characterize most of the region.

3. Eradicating poverty and discrimination. In spite of net economic growth in the 1990s, poverty and income concentration among the most wealthy both increased. There were more poor people in Latin America at the end of the 1990s than at the beginning, even as most governments' social spending (education, health, housing, and social security) increased.

4. Guaranteeing sustainable development and conserving the natural environment. There was virtually no progress beyond rhetorical commitments to environmental protection. In the 1990s, the region experienced further deterioration in environmental quality.

Preserving and Strengthening Democracy

For the first time in Latin America's turbulent political history, most countries in the region have had elected governments for the past 15–25 years. The challenge many face, however, is how to consolidate these formal democratic processes. This involves the difficult process of building both effective political institutions and a routinized and predictable process that can deal effectively with the growing array of citizen needs and demands.

Recognizing that a hemisphere of stable democratic states is in the best interests of the United States at various levels, the Clinton administration was committed to doing what it could to strengthen democratic practice in Latin America, as elsewhere. Nevertheless, a review of some important indicators of the level and quality of democracy between 1990 and 2000, such as political rights, civil liberties, and corruption, suggests that U.S. officials were less successful in meeting this goal during the Clinton years than they would have wished.

Because of the corrosive effects of drug production and trafficking on democracy, the SOA document included counter-drug policy within the strengthening democracy objective. Over the course of the 1990s, however, in spite of a major push by the U.S. government and its counterparts in major drug-producing countries, they failed to reduce areas of cultivation and quantities of cocaine and heroin and the corruption and violence associated with them. Counter-drug policy, then, provoked additional challenges for democratic practice rather than helping to strengthen it.

POLITICAL RIGHTS AND CIVIL LIBERTIES

One measure of the overall level of democracy in individual countries, though admittedly not finely calibrated, is the annual Freedom House rating of the level of political rights and civil liberties.[1] When the summary data for 1992 and 2001 for Latin America are examined to determine the changes that occurred in these two indicators of democracy over the course of the Clinton administration, there is little difference for the region as a whole (see table 5.1).

In both 1992, the year before President Clinton took office, and 2001, the year after he left, nine Latin American countries were classified by the Freedom House assessment as "Free," nine as "Partly Free," and two as "Not Free." Even so, there were, on balance, some overall improvements in political rights (three countries more up than down over the period) and in civil liberties (four more up than down), most notably in El Salvador, Mexico, Panama, and Peru. However, these cases were largely offset by deteriorating conditions in other Latin American nations, including Argentina, Brazil, Ecuador, and Honduras.

Furthermore, several countries experienced unorthodox, if not blatantly unconstitutional, regime changes in the face of internal crises and popular unrest between 1997 and 2000. There were two such shifts in Ecuador (1997 and 2000), one in Paraguay (1999), and one in Peru (2000). Turmoil that had been building for some time manifested itself in seven other cases of irregular changes of governments after Clinton left office—Argentina in 2001 and 2002, Venezuela in 2002, Bolivia in 2003 and 2005, Haiti in 2004, and Ecuador, again, in 2005.[2]

Certainly multiple factors, many of them internal and idiosyncratic, help to explain the erosion in the quality of democracy over the decade. Given the explicit goal of U.S. policy to strengthen democratic practice, however, and the sharp increases in both U.S. social and economic aid and military and police assistance for Latin America during the late 1990s (table 5.2), the results are disappointing. Unfortunately, stasis and slippage rather than progress toward more stable and consolidated elected governments in the region characterized the Clinton years.

Table 5.1 Political Rights and Civil Liberties in Latin America, 1992 and 2001

Country	Political rights[a]			Civil liberties			Freedom status[b]		
	1992	2001	Change[c]	1992	2001	Change[c]	1992	2001	Change[c]
Argentina	2	3	-	3	3	0	PF	PF	-
Bolivia	2	1	+	3	3	0	F	F	0
Brazil	2	3	-	3	3	0	F	PF	-
Chile	2	2	0	2	2	0	F	F	0
Colombia	2	4	-	4	4	0	PF	PF	0
Costa Rica	1	1	0	1	2	-	F	F	0
Cuba	7	7	0	7	7	0	NF	NF	0
Dominican Republic	2	2	0	3	2	+	F	F	0
Ecuador	2	3	-	3	3	0	F	PF	-
El Salvador	3	2	+	3	3	0	F	PF	-
Guatemala	4	3	+	5	4	+	PF	PF	0
Haiti	7	6	+	7	6	+	NF	NF	0
Honduras	2	3	-	3	3	0	F	PF	-
Mexico	4	2	+	3	3	0	PF	F	+
Nicaragua	4	3	+	3	3	0	PF	PF	0
Panama	4	1	+	3	2	+	PF	F	+
Paraguay	3	4	-	3	3	0	PF	PF	0
Peru	6	1	+	5	3	+	PF	F	+
Uruguay	1	1	0	2	1	+	F	F	0
Venezuela	3	3	0	3	5	-	PF	PF	0

Source: Freedom House, *Freedom in the World: Country Ratings 1972 through 2003* (New York: Freedom House, 2004), <freedomhouse.org/ratings/allscore04.xls> (July 22, 2005).

a. Numerical ratings range from 1 to 7 and are derived from a 10-question Political Rights (PR) checklist and a 15-question Civil Liberties (CL) list completed by some 30 analysts and advisors and complemented by outside news and other reports, contacts, and country visits, as well as discussions among regional analysts and specialists. For additional information, see Freedom House, *Freedom in the World 2003: Survey Methodology*, <freedomhouse.org/research/freeworld/2003/methodology.htm> (accessed July 23, 2005).

b. F = Free, PF = Partly Free, NF = Not Free. Final determination of F, PF, or NF status is based on overall point totals for the 10-question checklist for PR and the 15-question list for CL, in which each question receives 1–4 points. Totals of 68–100 = F, 34–67 = PF, and 0–33 = NF.

c. The overall pattern of the Freedom House indicators of political rights, civil liberties, and the status of freedom for Latin America as a whole shows a mixed pattern between 1992 and 2001. While half of the region's republics showed improvements in either political rights or civil liberties or both during this period, an equal number stayed the same or deteriorated. The overall pattern for the status of freedom remained unchanged, with as many countries judged as moving from partly free to free as moved in the opposite direction (four) and the rest staying the same (five F, five PF, and two NF).

Table 5.2. U.S. Security and Economic Assistance to Latin America and to Bolivia, Colombia, Mexico, and Peru, 1996–2000 (in millions of current dollars)

Year	Military/ police aid[a]	Total to BCMP[b]	Security aid to BCMP (%)	Social/ economic aid	Total to BCMP	Economic aid to BCMP (%)
1996	161	98	61	547	150[c]	27
1997	270	210	81	585	186	32
1998	298	210	70	634	185	29
1999	497	412	83	783	210	27
2000	977	889	91	953	497	52
Change (%)						
1996–2000	507	807	—	74	231	—

Source: Washington Office on Latin America (WOLA), Latin America Working Group Education Fund, and Center for International Policy, "U.S. Security and Economic Assistance to the Western Hemisphere," *Just the Facts: A Civilian's Guide to U.S. Defense and Security Assistance to Latin America and the Caribbean*, <www.ciponline.org/facts/country.htm> (April 15, 2005).
a. Both military/police aid and social/economic aid include assistance to Latin America and the Caribbean.
b. Bolivia, Colombia, Mexico, and Peru (BCMP) are the four major countries in Latin America that produce and traffic illegal drugs.
c. Between 1996 and 1998, Colombia received less than $1 million each year from the United States in social and economic aid as the result of the 1996–97 U.S. decertification of Columbia for not cooperating in counter-drug efforts.

CORRUPTION

The presence of corruption within elected governments reduces both their capacity to govern effectively and their legitimacy among the citizenry. While ascertaining levels of government corruption with any degree of certainty is a very difficult enterprise, the nongovernmental organization Transparency International (TI) has attempted to do so. Since 1995, TI has compiled annually from a number of surveys of businesspeople and country analysts a Corruption Perceptions Index (CPI) that provides their collective assessment of the degree of corruption they believe is present in the countries they follow most closely.

Although not complete due to the absence of a sufficient number of surveys for individual countries in some years, the information available for Latin America is quite disheartening (table 5.3). With only one consistent exception (Chile) and two others for some years (Costa Rica and Uruguay), Latin American countries cluster in the lower half of the nations covered by the annual CPI. Most have scores that are below 5 on a scale from 1 to 10, levels that for TI suggest perceptions of significant corruption by public of-

Table 5.3. Corruption Perceptions Index (CPI)[a] for Latin America, 1995–2002

Country[c]	1995	1996	1997	1998	1999	2000	2001	2002
Argentina	5.2	3.4	2.8	3.0	3.0	3.5	3.5	2.8
Bolivia	—	3.4	2.1	2.8	2.5	2.7	2.0	2.2
Brazil	2.7	3.0	3.6	4.0	4.1	3.9	4.0	4.0
Chile	7.9	6.8	6.1	6.8	6.9	7.4	7.5	7.5
Colombia	3.4	2.7	2.2	2.2	2.9	3.2	3.8	3.6
Costa Rica	—	—	6.5	5.6	5.1	5.4	4.5	4.5
Dominican Republic	—	—	—	—	—	—	3.1	3.5
Ecuador	—	3.2	—	2.3	2.4	2.6	2.3	2.2
El Salvador	—	—	—	3.6	3.9	4.1	3.6	3.4
Guatemala	—	—	—	3.1	3.2	—	2.9	2.5
Haiti	—	—	—	—	—	—	—	2.2
Honduras	—	—	—	1.7	1.8	—	2.7	2.7
Mexico	3.2	3.3	2.7	3.3	3.4	3.3	3.7	3.6
Nicaragua	—	—	—	3.0	3.1	—	2.4	2.5
Panama	—	—	—	—	—	—	3.7	3.0
Paraguay	—	—	—	1.5	2.0	—	—	1.7
Peru	—	—	—	4.5	4.5	4.4	4.1	4.0
Uruguay	—	—	4.1	4.3	4.4	—	5.1	5.1
Venezuela	2.7	2.5	2.8	2.3	2.6	2.7	2.8	2.5

Source: Transparency International, *Corruption Perceptions Index*, annual, 1995–2002, <www.transparency.org/cpi.en.html> (accessed July 22, 2005).

a. The CPI score ranges from 0 to 10, with higher scores indicating lower levels of perceived corruption. Each annual score is derived from a compilation of surveys by several independent institutions that were conducted over a three-year period among businesspeople, academics, and country analysts. They reflect their perceptions at the time of the survey of the level of corruption in the country or countries they follow. The number of surveys reviewed has ranged between 5 and 15, depending on the year, and the number of countries assessed worldwide has ranged between 41 and 102. No country is included without at least 3 surveys; for Latin America the number has varied between 3 and 10, with a tendency to increase over time, as it has for the rest of the world.

b. The number of countries in the CPI by year is 41 in 1995, 54 in 1996, 52 in 1997, 95 in 1998, 99 in 1999, 90 in 2000, 91 in 2001, and 102 in 2002. The CPI ranking worldwide for individual Latin American countries ranges from a high of 14 (Chile, 1995) to a low of 98 (Paraguay, 2002), with most countries most years in the bottom half of the rankings. Transparency International considers a CPI below 5 to reflect substantial levels of corruption among politicians and public officials. By this benchmark, only Chile has been consistently perceived to have relatively low levels of corruption.

c. Cuba is not included.

ficials. Equally if not even more telling is the downward trend over time for those Latin American governments for which longitudinal data are available. Although a few have registered slight improvements over time in their CPIs and Brazil and Uruguay have made considerable progress, fully two-thirds (12 of 18) experienced a decline in the CPI index between 1995 and 2002.

One of the conclusions of a report by the U.S. General Accounting Office on the overall effects of U.S. support for democracy-building initiatives in six Latin American countries that received the bulk of American economic and technical assistance between 1992 and 2002 (Bolivia, Colombia, El Salvador, Guatemala, Nicaragua, and Peru) is that "the results of anticorruption programs have been modest so far. . . . Projects have been hindered by politicization and a lack of consistent political support." The report's authors believe that "it is unlikely that U.S. governance-related assistance will be able to produce sustainable results without ongoing, long-term involvement."[3]

Many factors contribute to corruption among political elites, including long-standing internal practices, personal values, the absence of effective enforcement, and a degree of public tolerance, if not acceptance. However, the persistence of high levels of perceived corruption in most Latin American countries during a period in which the U.S. government was providing substantial assistance, with an emphasis on adherence to the rule of law as a key component of its goal of strengthening democracy, also points up the failure of the Clinton administration to contribute to the advance of effective democratic governance in the region.

DRUG PRODUCTION AND TRAFFICKING

Some Latin American countries have been major producers of illegal drugs for U.S. consumers for more than three decades. The Andean region is the world's only source of coca leaf, the raw material for cocaine, and such countries as Mexico and Colombia also provide a portion of the heroin and marijuana consumed in the United States. As part of its overall counter-drug strategy, successive U.S. governments have pursued crop eradication, interdiction, and legal crop substitution policies in their efforts to reduce the supply of drugs reaching the United States.[4]

The drug trade and the U.S. response to it also have had a significant impact on the producing countries in the region. Although tens of thousands of small farmers and their families benefit from the cash income they receive for their coca, opium poppy, and marijuana crops, the main beneficiaries are the drug manufacturers and traffickers. The drug trade also generates significant corruption and violence, with major negative impacts on the ability of elected officials in affected countries to govern effectively. Such a connection explains the inclusion of a component in the Miami SOA Plan of Action that considers drug production and trafficking reduction within the strengthening of democracy objective.

Particularly during Clinton's second term, the U.S. government committed significant new resources to the counter-drug campaign. Military and police assistance increased fivefold between 1996 and 2000, and economic and social aid grew by 74 percent (table 5.2). While almost every Latin American and Caribbean country received some of these new funds, governments of the major illegal drug-producing and trafficking nations—Bolivia, Colombia, Mexico, and Peru—garnered the largest share. Between 1996 and 2000, the share of total U.S. support for the region going to these four countries increased from 59 to 91 percent of military and police aid and from 27 to 52 percent of social and economic aid.

In spite of such a significant U.S. effort in the late 1990s, the impact on drug production was modest indeed. Estimates of hectares of coca leaf cultivation in Bolivia, Colombia, and Peru combined did show a 12 percent decline between 1996 and 2001, in the context of an expansion of coca leaf eradication by some 323 percent over these same years (table 5.4). In spite of such major eradication efforts, however, total potential cocaine production actually grew by 9 percent over this period. Opium poppy cultivation (for the production of heroin) and potential yield in Colombia and Mexico showed a similar pattern, with a 4 percent decline in estimated hectares between 1996 and 2001 but a 16 percent increase in total production (table 5.4, note a).

On balance, the Clinton administration failed to support and strengthen democracy in Latin America by reducing illegal drug supplies of cocaine and heroin in order to counterbalance their corrosive effects on democratic institutions through corruption and criminal activity. Cocaine production estimates actually increased during Clinton's years in office, and opium yield estimates, though declining significantly over the eight years, rebounded after 1996. In all four major drug-producing countries, the CPI remained at levels that suggested the presence of significant corruption, even though some improvement was noted in Colombia and Mexico between 1996 and 2001 (table 5.3). The civil liberties scale showed no improvement over the period, while the gains registered in political rights in Bolivia, Mexico, and Peru can be attributed to a variety of factors unrelated to U.S. counter-drug policies.[5]

Promoting Prosperity through Economic Integration and Free Trade

In the aftermath of the extended economic crisis in Latin America in the 1980s, most of the now elected governments in the region decided to adopt economic liberalization reforms as a way to restore economic growth. En-

Table 5.4. Drug Production in Bolivia, Colombia, and Peru, 1992–2001[a]

Country	1992	1993	1994	1995	1996	1997	1998	1999	2000	2001	Change (%)
Net coca cultivation (in thousands of hectares)											
Bolivia	45.0	47.2	48.1	48.6	48.1	45.8	38.0	21.8	14.8	19.9	-56
Colombia	37.1	39.7	44.7	50.9	67.2	79.5	101.8	122.5	136.2	169.8	+358
Peru	129.1	108.8	108.6	115.3	94.4	68.8	51.0	38.7	34.1	34.0	-74
Totals	211.2	195.7	201.4	214.8	209.7	194.1	190.8	183	185.1	223.7	+6
Net coca eradication (in thousands of hectares)											
Bolivia	3.2	2.4	1.1	5.5	7.5	7.0	11.6	17.0	7.7	9.4	+190
Colombia	1.0	.8	4.9	8.8	5.6	19.0	—	43.2	47.0	84.3	+8,333
Peru	0	0	0	0	1.3	3.5	7.8	13.8	6.2	3.9	+163
Totals	4.2	3.2	6.0	14.3	14.4	29.6	19.4	54.0	60.9	97.6	+2,224
Potential cocaine production (in metric tons)											
Bolivia	225	240	255	240	215	200	150	70	43	60	-73
Colombia	60	65	70	230	300	350	435	520	580	839	+1,298
Peru	550	410	435	460	435	325	240	175	154	140	-75
Totals	835	715	760	930	950	875	835	765	777	1,039	+24[b]

Sources: U.S. Department of State, Bureau for International Narcotics and Law Enforcement Affairs, International Narcotics Control Strategy (INCSR) Report, 2000; INSCR Report, 2001; INSCR Report, 2003, <www.state.gov/g/inl/nrcrpt/2000/888.htm> (July 24, 2005).

a. Latin America produces all of the world's cocaine (almost entirely in Bolivia, Colombia, and Peru) and small portions of opium (heroin) and marijuana (mostly in Colombia and Mexico). Net opium poppy cultivation in Colombia and Mexico declined from 23,300 hectares in 1992 to 10,900 in 2001. Some 19,800 hectares of opium poppy were eradicated in 1992, and 21,700 in 2001, an increase of 10%. The potential yield of opium gum also decreased, from 240 metric tons in 1992 to 136 in 2001 (39%). Net marijuana cultivation also decreased over these years, from 20,400 hectares to 8,900 (56%). However, overall potential yield increased during the same period, from 9,500 metric tons to 11,200 (18%). INCSR Reports, 2000–2003.

b. Potential production of cocaine in Bolivia, Colombia, and Peru, as of 2003, had declined to 771 metric tons, a drop of 8% from 1992 figures and 26% from 2001, entirely from reductions in Colombia. INSCR Report, 2003.

Table 5.5. U.S. trade with Mexico and Latin America, 1988–2001 (in billions of current dollars)

Year	Mexico Exports	Latin American trade (%) Imports	Latin America (except Cuba) Exports	World trade (%) Imports	Exports	Imports	Exports	Imports
1988	20.6	23.3	52	48	40.1	48.9	12.5	11.1
1989	25.0	27.2	56	50	44.4	54.8	12.2	11.6
1990	28.3	30.2	57	49	49.5	61.0	12.6	12.3
1991	33.3	31.1	57	52	58.9	59.5	14.0	12.2
1992	40.6	35.2	57	54	71.3	65.5	15.9	12.3
1993	41.6	39.9	57	56	73.3	71.3	15.8	12.3
1994	50.8	49.5	60	58	87.8	85.7	17.1	12.8
1995	46.3	62.1	51	61	90.7	101.3	15.5	13.6
1996	56.8	74.3	55	62	103.7	119.8	16.6	15.1
1997	71.3	85.9	56	63	127.9	135.9	18.6	15.6
1998	79.0	94.7	58	67	135.6	142.0	19.9	15.6
1999	86.9	109.7	64	67	135.9	164.4	19.5	16.0
2000	111.3	135.9	68	67	163.7	203.3	20.9	16.7
2001	101.3	131.3	66	68	152.7	193.4	20.9	16.9
Change (%)								
1988–1992	+97	+51	—	—	+78	+34	—	—
1992–2000	+174	+286	—	—	+130	+211	—	—
1994–2000	+119	+175	—	—	+86	+140	—	—
1988–2001	+391	+464	—	—	+281	+295	—	—

Sources: 1988, U.S. Department of Commerce, *Statistical Abstract of the United States (SAUS) 1990*, table 1406, 806; 1989–92, *SAUS 1993*, table 1351, 813–17; 1993–94, *SAUS 1995*, table 1341, 819–822; 1995–98, *SAUS 1999*, table 1328, 805–8; 1999–2001, *SAUS 2004–05*, table 1298, 814–817, <www.census.gov/prod2/statcomp/documents/1990–01.pdf> (August 1, 2005).

couraged by the United States and International Financial Institutions in the context of the Washington Consensus, they reduced tariff barriers to open up trade and ended many private investment restrictions to foster an influx of new capital.

In the more open economy that emerged in most of Latin America over the course of the late 1980s and 1990s, both U.S. trade with the region and investment there expanded markedly. By 2001, U.S. exports to Latin America and imports from the region had increased almost threefold from their 1988 levels and represented a steadily growing share of U.S. global trade (table 5.5). U.S. direct investment in Latin America grew from just over $35 billion in 1998 to almost $139 billion by 2001 (table 5.6). The market reforms that opened up new opportunities for trade and investment and the responses they generated from both international and domestic private sectors contributed to Latin America's net economic growth during the 1990s.

Table 5.6. U.S. Direct Investment in Mexico and Latin America, 1988–2001 (in billions of current dollars)

Year	Mexico	Latin American investment (%)	Latin America (except Cuba)	World investment (%)
1988	5.7	16.2	35.3	10.5
1989	7.3	18.2	40.0	10.8
1990	10.3	23.5	43.9	10.2
1991	12.5	25.4	49.2	10.5
1992	13.7	24.9	55.1	11.0
1993	15.2	25.2	60.3	10.7
1994	17.0	24.9	68.0	11.1
1995	16.9	20.3	83.0	11.9
1996	19.4	20.3	95.4	12.0
1997	24.2	20.7	116.6	13.5
1998	26.7	20.6	129.3	12.9
1999	37.2	23.5	158.2	13.0
2000	39.4	24.7	159.2	12.1
2001	52.5	37.9	138.6	9.5
Change (%)				
1988–92	+140	—	+56	—
1992–2000	+589	—	+351	—
1994–2000	+132	—	+134	—
1988–2001	+820	—	+292	—

Sources: 1988–89, U.S. Department of Commerce, *Statistical Abstract of the United States (SAUS) 1990*, table 1338, 801; 1990–91, *SAUS 1993*, table 1329, 809; 1992–97, *SAUS 1999*, table 1317, 797; 1998–2001, *SAUS 2004–05*, table 1288, 806, <www.census.gov/prod2/statcomp/documents/1990–01.pdf> (August 1, 2005).

The negotiation and ratification of the North American Free Trade Agreement in 1993 was viewed as the first major step toward the economic integration of the hemisphere through what was to be the Free Trade Area of the Americas (FTAA). Its formal articulation at the 1994 SOA reflected an unusual consensus among all participants on the importance of this initiative and the need to move forward with its implementation.

The promise and potential benefits of the FTAA may be seen in Mexico's trade and investment expansion, which took place within NAFTA between 1995 and 2000. Mexico accounted for fully 75 percent of the increase in Latin American exports to the United States ($87 of $117 billion), as well as for 80 percent of U.S. export expansion to the region ($60 of $75 billion) during the first six years NAFTA was in effect (table 5.5). Although the increase in U.S. investment in Mexico from 1994 through 2000, compared with Latin America as a whole, was less dramatic ($22 of $91 billion, or 24 percent), in 2001 this proportion increased substantially ($36 of $71 billion, or 51 percent) (table 5.6).

Between 1998 and 2001, trade between Mexico and the United States increased on average by about 10 percent per year, more rapidly than for all of Latin America, and U.S. investment rose at more than twice the rate in Mexico than in the rest of the region. While Mexico's proximity to the United States and its relatively early market liberalizing reforms undoubtedly affect these differences, NAFTA's role is also an important factor.

Unfortunately, the promise of the FTAA as laid out in the Miami SOA was not to be realized, much to the disappointment of the Latin American heads of state who had committed a great deal of their political capital to the enterprise. The Clinton administration was divided on the issue on domestic political and substantive grounds.

With the fissures created within the Democratic Party over the bruising battle to win ratification of NAFTA, the president and his political advisors did not feel that they could press for Fast Track renewal without incurring even greater political fallout within their own party's ranks. The Republican majority in Congress, relishing the political benefits of the Democrats' divisions, refused to give the president a victory on the issue, even though most supported the free trade objective. Both Department of the Treasury and Office of the U.S. Trade Representative officials disagreed on the value of pursuing the FTAA and Fast Track, as their foot-dragging on an agreement for the SOA demonstrated.[6]

President Clinton himself, having led the charge for NAFTA ratification and for a successful SOA that included the FTAA, was not prepared to exercise his leadership in their aftermaths to ensure that promises turned into deeds. On balance, then, the progress that occurred during his two terms in office on both economic integration and free trade, though considerable, came about largely through advances in NAFTA and the U.S. private sector's role in pursuing the trade and investment opportunities available after the Latin American governments' own economic reforms. U.S. leadership, though at one point poised to take advantage of the historic opportunity that was then available, failed to follow through.[7]

Eradicating Poverty and Discrimination

Clearly, any official commitment to eliminate poverty and discrimination in Latin America, as the U.S. government and its counterparts in the region stated as a goal of the Miami summit, is a long-term project that cannot be achieved in just a few years. Furthermore, any reduction in either that might result during the course of a U.S. administration would come about through the interplay of a variety of factors, from internal manifestations of political

Table 5.7. Poverty and Indigence in Latin America, 1980–2002ᵃ (in millions of people, 19 countries not including Cuba)

Year	Poorᵇ Number	Population (%)	Indigent Number	Population (%)	Total Number	Population (%)
1980	73.5	21.9	62.4	18.6	135.9	40.5
1990	106.8	25.8	93.4	22.5	200.2	48.3
1997	115.0	24.5	88.8	19.0	203.8	43.5
1999	122.0	25.3	89.4	18.5	211.4	43.8
2000	118.7	24.4	88.4	18.1	207.1	42.5
2001	122.2	24.7	91.7	18.5	213.9	43.2
2002	124.0	24.6	97.4	19.4	221.4	44.0
Change (%)						
1990–2001	+14.4	-4.3	-1.8	-17.7	+6.8	-10.6

Source: Economic Commission for Latin America and the Caribbean, *Social Panorama of Latin America 2002–2003*, UN Pub. LC/G 2209–P (Santiago, Chile: UN Publications, May 2004), tables I.2 and I.3, 50.

a. This table is based on country-by-country tabulations of household survey data. For population percentages of poverty and indigence by specific country, 1990–2002, see source cited, table I.4, 54–55.

b. Poverty is defined in terms of a per capita income by household below what members must have to meet their basic nutritional and nonnutritional needs; indigence, below what is needed to meet nutritional needs only. For further discussion, see source cited, box I.1, 51–52.

will within the countries to the interaction of international economic institutions and market forces. In addition, the indicators available to measure levels of poverty and discrimination are incomplete and imprecise.

In spite of these important caveats, however, it should be possible to make some preliminary and tentative assessments of progress accomplished during the Clinton years in reducing poverty and discrimination in Latin America. The data available suggest that the record on lowering levels of poverty over the course of the 1990s is a mixed one.

The positive news is that the proportion of the population of Latin America below the poverty line declined by over 10 percent between 1990 and 2001. The indigent among them fell even more, by almost 18 percent. Over the same period, however, the total number in poverty increased by almost 14 million, or 7 percent, from 200 million to almost 214 million (table 5.7). Unemployment rates also increased markedly and continuously, almost doubling from 4.6 percent in 1990 to 8.6 percent in 1999.[8]

Over roughly the same period, income inequality within the countries of the region, measured by the proportion of total income held by the richest

Table 5.8. Income Inequality in Latin America, 1989–2002[a] (17 countries,[b] by percentage of total income, richest 10%)

Country	First measurement (1989–93)[c]	Last measurement (2000–2002)	Change (%)
Argentina	34.8	42.1	+21.0
Bolivia	38.2	41.1	+7.6
Brazil	43.9	46.8	+6.6
Chile	40.7	40.3	-1.0
Colombia	41.8 (1994)	39.1	-6.5
Costa Rica	25.6	30.2	+18.0
Ecuador	30.5	34.3	+12.5
El Salvador	32.9 (1995)	33.3	+1.2
Guatemala	40.6	36.8	-9.4
Honduras	43.1	39.4	-8.6
Mexico	36.6	33.2	-9.3
Nicaragua	38.4	40.7	+6.0
Panama	34.2	32.7	-4.4
Paraguay	28.9 (1997)	37.3	+29.1
Peru	33.3	33.5	+1.0
Uruguay	31.2	27.3	-12.5
Venezuela	28.7	31.3	+9.1
Latin American average	35.5	36.4	+2.5

Source: ECLAC, *Social Panorama of Latin America 2002–2003*, UN Pub. LC/G 2209–P (Santiago, Chile: UN Publications, May 2004), table I.6, 73–74.
a. This table is based on country-by-country tabulation of household survey data.
b. Cuba, the Dominican Republic, and Haiti are not included.
c. Methodology and qualifications are noted in the source cited, box I.7, 78.

decile of the population, increased from 35.5 percent to 36.4 percent (table 5.8). Improvements in wealth distribution in such countries as Uruguay, Guatemala, Honduras, and Mexico were more than offset by increased concentration in others, including Paraguay, Argentina, Costa Rica, Ecuador, Brazil, and Bolivia.

The failure to make the progress desired in reducing poverty or income distribution inequality occurred in spite of significant increases in both social spending by most Latin American countries (table 5.9) and outlays of U.S. economic and social assistance during the decade (table 5.2). The major increases in U.S. trade with Latin America and direct investment in the region were also insufficient to have any material effect on the number in poverty or income distribution. The overall result, then, was the persistence of unacceptably high levels of poverty as well as some further concentration of income among the already wealthy, along with steady increases in unemployment. These outcomes were at odds with the Clinton administration's commitment to improving the well-being of Latin America's citizens.

Table 5.9. Social Spending in Latin America, 1990–2001 (18 countries[a] in 1997 dollars)

Years	Total social spending[b] per capita	Public spending (%)	Education spending per capita	Health spending per capita
1990–91	342	41.5	—	—
1992–93	399	43.5	—	—
1994–95	404	45.2	—	—
1996–97	432	45.8	118	95
1998–99	470	46.1	—	—
2000–2001	494	48.4	139	110
Change (%)				
1990–2001	+44	+16.6	+18 (1996–2001)	+16 (1996–2001)

Source: ECLAC, *Social Panorama of Latin America 2002–2003*, UN Pub. LC/G 2209–P (Santiago, Chile: UN Publications, May 2004), table IV.1, 175; table IV.3, 178; table IV.4, 184; table IV.5, 185.

a. Cuba and Haiti are not included.

b. Includes government spending for education, health, housing, and social security.

The question of discrimination is subject to the same qualifications as for poverty, income inequality, and unemployment. In this area, however, progress during the 1990s characterized most areas measured that relate to gender discrimination. Female employment increased by almost 2 percent between 1990 and 1999, and female education levels among the economically active also advanced, especially among the university educated (table 5.10). The only disquieting note is the increase in female unemployment over the decade, which more than doubled, from 5.1 percent in 1990 to 11.2 percent in 1999. This suggests that, as more women entered the workplace, an increasing number were unable to find or maintain full-time employment.

The representation of women in elected positions in Latin American legislatures showed increases between 1990 and 2000 in almost every country studied, more than doubling in Argentina, Brazil, Colombia, Ecuador, Paraguay, and Uruguay (table 5.11). While a variety of factors contributed to this positive development, including the institution of party list quotas by several Latin American governments, there is little doubt that the greater attention to the issue by U.S. officials stimulated a heightened awareness among their counterparts in the region.

Table 5.10. Gender Discrimination Indicators in Latin America, 1990–2002 (15 countries,[a] national totals, in percentages)

Year	Female employment (%)	Female unemployment (% of Economically Active)	Female years of education 0–5	6–9	10–12	13+
1990	31.5	5.1	28.0	30.3	39.8	36.7
1994	32.4	7.2	29.8	30.6	38.9	37.0
1997	33.1	8.7	30.1	31.1	38.0	40.8
1999	33.4	11.2	30.3	31.0	38.1	41.1
2002	38.4	11.1	35.8	35.1	41.3	45.5
Change (%)						
1990–99	+6.0	+119.6	+8.2	+2.3	-4.3	+12.0

Source: ECLAC, *Social Panorama of Latin America, 2002–2003*, UN Pub. LC/G 2209–P (Santiago, Chile: UN Publications, May 2004), table III.5b, 158.
a. Cuba, the Dominican Republic, Guatemala, Haiti, and Venezuela are not included.

Table 5.11. Percentage of Women in National Legislatures in Latin America, 1980, 1990, 2000[a]

Country	1980[b]	1990	2000
Argentina	11	14	30
Bolivia	9	13	16
Brazil	2	5	13
Chile	8	12	15
Colombia	6	10	25
Costa Rica	9	12	19
Dominican Republic	20	12	23
Ecuador	0	7	15
Mexico	15	31	32
Nicaragua	12	19	10
Paraguay	6	10	21
Uruguay	1	6	22
Venezuela	5	10	10
Average	8	12	19

Source: ECLAC, *Social Panorama of Latin America, 2002–2003*, UN Pub. LC/G 2209–P (Santiago, Chile: UN Publications, May 2004), table III.10, 169.
a. Percentages shown in the table are the sum of the percentages of elected female legislators in both houses where bicameral legislatures exist (all except Ecuador, Nicaragua, and Venezuela, which have unicameral legislatures).
b. Except for Chile (1970) and Uruguay (1972).

Guaranteeing Sustainable Development and Conserving the Environment

Environmental issues reflected important differences in perspectives between the U.S. government and most of its Latin American counterparts. For some years U.S. officials had viewed with growing alarm the progressive erosion of forest cover in the region, particularly in the Amazon, and the increasing production of greenhouse gases there, especially carbon dioxide, which were contributing to the depletion of the ozone layer over Antarctica and southern South America. They urged Latin American governments to take steps to reduce and control the degradation of the environment in their countries. However, at important gatherings to address such issues, such as the "Earth Summit" in Rio de Janeiro in 1992, Bush administration representatives were unwilling to provide the financial support necessary to assist their counterparts in dealing with the problem or to back a multilateral initiative that was to deal with environmental issues on a global level.[9]

From the Latin American perspective, developed countries in general and the United States in particular were responsible for most of the environmental degradation that was occurring, particularly in levels of air pollution. Therefore, the developed countries' governments were the ones who needed to set specific standards for its reduction. Although the European countries agreed, the Bush administration did not. Since all participants at the Rio summit needed to sign on to any such accord, U.S. reluctance ensured that no progress was made there on this important environmental issue.

With Clinton's electoral victory and arrival in the White House, most expected a much greater concern for environmental issues during his administration. His vice president, Al Gore, joined him with a reputation as a strong advocate for environmental protection. Clinton's insistence on an environmental side agreement for the NAFTA treaty seemed to demonstrate the administration's commitment. Nevertheless, the specifics of the agreement failed to provide an effective enforcement mechanism and relied on individual governments to implement environmental policy change.[10] While the side agreements on the environment and labor helped to mollify some members of Congress and secure NAFTA's ratification, then, they lacked the teeth required to make them effective instruments in practice.

As the preparations for the first SOA took shape, they offered a new opportunity to make environmental issues a major focus. Gore succeeded in his insistence that one of its specific objectives be sustainable development and improvement in the quality of the environment, a goal that was supported by the heads of state at the Miami gathering.[11] Although the com-

Table 5.12. Environmental indicators for Latin America, 1990 and 2000 (in thousands of hectares—ha, tons—tn, cubic meters—m³, or people, 17 countriesª)

Indicator	1990	2000	Change (%)
Total forest area (ha)	1,005,469	958,647	-4.7
Total wood production			
(industrial, fuel, charcoal, in m³)	349,594	427,324	+22.2
Air pollution (total CO_2 emissions, in tons)	843,997	1,138,900	+34.9
Fertilizer use (tons)	6,792	12,855	+89.3
Protected forests			
Total number	1,436	2,162	+50.6
Area (ha)	146,374	200,729	+37.1
	1990	1998	Change (%)
Access to potable water			
Rural population	73,508	71,465	-2.8
Percentage	63.7	61.4	-3.6
Urban population	253,067	340,374	+34.5
Percentage	86.3	93.2	+8.0

Source: United Nations Environment Program, *Global Environmental Outlook (GEO): Latin America and the Caribbean, 2003* (San José, Costa Rica: UNEP, November 2003), 258–60, 262, 270–72, 274, <www.mirror.unep.org/geo/pdfs/GEO_lac2003English.pdf> (accessed August 7, 2005).
a. Cuba, the Dominican Republic, and Haiti are not included.

mitment to improvement in environmental quality in the hemisphere was reiterated at an environmental summit in Santa Cruz, Bolivia, in 1996 and at the second SOA in Santiago, Chile, in 1998, the record of change in key environmental indicators in Latin America between 1990 and 2000 suggests that deeds failed to match rhetoric (table 5.12).

Air pollution, as measured by total carbon dioxide emissions, increased over the decade by almost 35 percent, while the region's total forested area continued to be depleted at a rate that was twice that of the rest of the world.[12] Tree cutting for industry, fuel, and charcoal grew by about 22 percent between 1990 and 2000, while fertilizer application, which also contributes to pollution, almost doubled.

Progress was made in protecting some forested areas during these years, however. The number of protected forest areas increased by 726, or almost 51 percent, and the total area protected grew by more than 54 million hectares. Even so, protected forests still accounted for less than 21 percent of the total forested area in Latin America, and most lacked the government budget or personnel needed to ensure enforcement of their status from the encroachments of loggers and farmers.[13]

Progress was also made in the 1990s in providing Latin America's population with access to potable water, especially in urban areas, which reached over 93 percent by 1998, an increase of over 87 million people. However, rural residents did not receive similar benefits and even declined slightly in the proportion served and in total numbers (table 5.12).

Many factors contributed to this overall lack of advancement in improving environmental quality in Latin America during the 1990s. These included the pressures associated with economic growth and foreign trade expansion, the efforts of millions of poor farmers to eke out a living by accessing new land, and the limited ability of governments to enforce environmental legislation. However, U.S. environmental policy during the Clinton years also contributed to this failure.

The commitment in principle was not matched with specific measures or financial resources.[14] A failure to enact more stringent environmental controls at home, the largest single source of the world's air pollution, made it more difficult to press for them in the less developed economies of Latin America. The U.S. goal of expanding regional trade, for all of its benefits, put new pressure on the region's governments to exploit their countries' resources rather than to conserve them. On balance, top U.S. officials failed to provide the leadership necessary on the regional environment improvement objective to make the progress they envisioned become a reality.

Conclusions

As the discussion above indicates, the Clinton administration was not able to advance very far in accomplishing its major policy goals toward Latin America as articulated in the SOA Declaration of Principles. While this may be due in part to the goals' overly ambitious nature, the lack of progress also suggests the presence of a variety of inhibiting factors. More often than not, the multiple challenges to implementing an effective and coherent policy toward the region limited policy makers' abilities to accomplish their objectives and produced less than satisfactory results.

The Clinton years were marked by a number of quiet and cumulative successes, related primarily to continuing or following through on the positive initiatives of the Bush administration, from the Brady Plan to NAFTA. Other successes derived from effective responses to unanticipated events, as with Mexico's peso crisis and the Ecuador-Peru border war. The administration was also able to forge a new regional multilateral forum for dealing with common concerns in the SOAs, an initiative that also demonstrated leadership's ability to coordinate the U.S. foreign policy bureaucracy and to engage in effective consultation with its Latin American counterparts. Such successes indicate that those responsible for regional policy during

Table 5.13. U.S. Department of State (DOS) and Federal Government Budget
Outlays, 1989–2001 (in billions of current dollars)

Fiscal year	Federal budget	Change (%)	DOS budget	Change (%)
1989	1,143.7	—	4.58	—
1990	1,253.2	+10	4.80	+5
1991	1,324.4	+6	5.15	+7
1992	1,381.7	+4	5.94	+15
1993	1,409.5	+2	6.41	+8
1994	1,461.9	+4	6.80	+4
1995	1,515.8	+4	6.27	-8
1996	1,652.6	+9	5.74	-8
1997	1,601.3	+3	6.03	+5
1998	1,652.6	+3	5.38	-11
1999	1,702.9	+3	6.46	+20
2000	1,788.8	+5	6.85	+6
1993–2000	446.7	+32	0.44	+7
2001 est.	1,856.2	+4	9.30	+36

Source: Data from U.S. Government, "Historical Tables," *Budget of the United States Government, Fiscal Year 2002* (Washington, D.C.: Government Printing Office, 2001), table 4.1, Outlays by Agency: 1962–2006, 73–75.

the Clinton years had a vision of what needed to be accomplished and the capacity to make difficult decisions at times to deal effectively with a number of important problems.

At the same time, however, a variety of constraints limited the ability of the Clinton administration to achieve its major goals in Latin American policy. These related primarily to leadership perceptions and priorities, the multiple consequences of external events, tensions between domestic politics and foreign policy, and conflicting policy priorities in the region.

Major problems in other parts of the world often took priority over regional issues. Key policy makers, including the president and his secretaries of state, had little interest in or commitment to Latin America. Those policy makers who were responsible for the region often found that they had insufficient support or confidence from their superiors, thereby limiting their ability to operate effectively.[15] The progressive and cumulative reduction in Department of State resources, besides its demoralizing effect on career professionals, eroded the government's institutional capacity to deal effectively with policy issues.

After a significant increase in Department of State (DOS) budget outlays during the George H. W. Bush administration, spending declined substantially over the course of the Clinton years (table 5.13). When inflation rates are taken into account, the DOS budget increased by 11 percent between

1989 and 1992, but declined by about 16 percent between 1993 and 2000.[16] The erosion was particularly marked over the course of Clinton's first term, some 22 percent, although DOS outlays did rebound by about 7 percent in inflation-adjusted dollars during his second term. The overall decline in the DOS budget between 1993 and 2000 occurred even as total federal government expenditures were increasing, after inflation is taken into account, by about 4 percent.

These disquieting DOS budget figures were also reflected in employment trends within the U.S. government's foreign affairs community. Department employees were reduced by over 1,100 between 1994 and 1996, or by more than 4 percent. The impact on other agencies was even greater, with the U.S. Information Agency (USIA) losing about 13 percent of its staff and the U.S. Agency for International Development (USAID) shedding almost 20 percent of its employees during this period.[17]

The failure to provide the resources and staff necessary to keep pace with rapidly increasing U.S. government worldwide responsibilities during a particularly critical period reflected poorly on both the executive and legislative branches. True, this pattern of insufficient funding for foreign affairs is a long-standing one and reflects a preoccupation with domestic concerns.[18] Nevertheless, the unwillingness of top officials in both branches during the Clinton presidency to push for significant increases in funding to take advantage of a favorable international environment represented a major failure of political leadership. As a result, the lack of sufficient resources served as a significant constraint on the U.S. government's ability to accomplish its ambitious foreign policy objectives in Latin America, as elsewhere in the world.

The shift to a Republican-controlled Congress that was much more interested in domestic concerns and had a deep animus toward Clinton significantly increased tension between the legislative and executive branches. Congress's decision to impeach Clinton began a drawn-out if ultimately unsuccessful process that virtually immobilized top leadership capacity to follow through on foreign policy issues for more than a year. In addition, significant differences between the two branches also expressed themselves in such specific areas as appointments, drug policy, and Cuba.

Multiple domestic pressures also affected the priorities of the administration in the region, most particularly in the tension between advancing on the counter-drug production and trafficking front on the one hand, and enhancing democratic procedures and practices on the other. Policies toward Peru in the late 1990s illustrated the challenges faced and the negative consequences of the decisions made.

The overall result of the interplay of these multiple constraints and policy leadership perceptions and priorities was to limit in various ways the ability of the Clinton administration to pursue effectively the vision and goals of its Latin American policy agenda. These limitations significantly inhibited the policy makers' ability to take full advantage of the favorable circumstances in the region that were initially available to them. Accomplishments and continuities were too often offset by reactive and ad hoc responses that conveyed the impression of a policy adrift.

On balance, although the Clinton administration may be credited with policy successes in several discrete areas, from NAFTA ratification and the Mexican peso crisis response, to the Guatemalan peace agreement and the Ecuador-Peru border dispute resolution, among others, it lost a major opportunity to build a coherent and comprehensive policy toward Latin America. Multiple constraints and unanticipated events limited the space available to forge effective policies, and exercises of effective and decisive leadership, though present on occasion, were too few and far between to break through the barriers they posed. By squandering the opening provided by a felicitous convergence of forces in the late 1980s and early 1990s, President Clinton and his advisors contributed to renewed disquiet in the region over U.S. policy intentions as well as the seriousness of its commitment to Latin America.

Notes

Chapter 1. Clinton's Latin American Policies in Context: The Concerns and the Approach

1. *Latin America* usually refers to the 20 independent countries south of the United States that were once colonies of Spain (18), Portugal (1), or France (1). This designation includes three countries in the Caribbean (Cuba, the Dominican Republic, and Haiti) and is the one used in this text. The Caribbean usually refers to the independent countries that once formed part of the British (12) and Dutch (1) empires that are in or that border on the Caribbean Sea or the Gulf of Mexico, but often includes the dependent territories in the region as well as the three nations noted above.

2. Huntington, *The Third Wave*, provides a worldwide perspective on the democratization phenomenon in the late twentieth century and the historical context. For a summary of the "waves," or historical cycles of authoritarianism and democracy in Latin America, see Palmer, "The Military in Latin America," 326–35.

3. Among other recent studies addressing the trajectory of Latin American politics and its contemporary elements, see Smith, *Democracy in Latin America*, esp. 213–62, and Peeler, *Building Democracy*, esp. 141–64.

4. As laid out in the "Declaration of Principles," in Feinberg, *Summitry in the Americas*, appendix D, 213–17.

5. Among others, Peeler, *Building Democracy*, 164–66; Smith, *Democracy in Latin America*, 332–37.

6. United Nations Economic Commission for Latin America and the Caribbean (ECLAC), *A Decade of Light and Shadow*, 99–128, 231–42.

7. ECLAC, *Social Panorama of Latin America, 2002–2003*, 50, 73–74, 158, 169, 175, 178, 184, 185.

8. United Nations Environment Program, *Global Environmental Outlook*, 258, 260, 270, 272.

9. Among others, Pastor, *Exiting the Whirlpool*, 109–10.

10. Numerous comments by career foreign policy officials interviewed by the author in Washington in 2001 and 2002 noted on this problem and the degree to which they felt constrained in their ability to follow through on specific policies toward the region.

11. See table 5.13 for details on the annual budget of the Department of State.

12. The issues raised in these policy areas are among those considered in some detail in the cases discussed in chapter 4.

13. The case of U.S. policy toward Peru in the late 1990s highlights the problem of choosing between these two desirable objectives and is developed in chapter 4.

14. Morganthau, *Politics among Nations.*
15. Allison, *Essence of Decision*, 144–84.
16. Robert Putnam, "Diplomacy and Domestic Politics," 427–32.
17. Wittkopf, *Domestic Sources of American Foreign Policy*, 3–9 and fig. I.1, 4.
18. Milner, *Interests, Institutions, and Information*, 4–5.
19. As developed, e.g., in Schoultz, *Beneath the United States.*

Chapter 2. The Changing International and Regional Context of Inter-American Relations

1. Kennan, "Latin America," 177–88.
2. Wood, *Dismantling of the Good Neighbor Policy*, esp. 190–209.
3. Schoultz, *Beneath the United States*, 332–66.
4. Immerman, *CIA in Guatemala*. The U.S. covert initiative in Guatemala was a major turning point in U.S. policy toward Latin America. The most prevalent interpretation of the intervention is that it was designed to protect U.S. business interests in Guatemala, specifically the United Fruit Company. However, within weeks of Arbenz's replacement by the compliant Col. Carlos Castillo Armas, the U.S. attorney general brought an antitrust suit in federal court against United Fruit for monopolizing foreign trade. This action marked the beginning of the end of the company's dominance in Guatemala. Schlesinger and Kinzer, *Bitter Fruit*, 229. The message that the Dwight D. Eisenhower administration (1953–61) appeared to be sending, in bringing forward the suit against United Fruit at this time (a suit originally prepared by the Harry Truman administration [1945–53]), was that its primary goal in Latin America generally, and Guatemala in particular, was to root out communism, not to protect U.S. business.
5. Schlesinger and Kinzer, *Bitter Fruit*, 228–29. One result of this dramatic failure was to seal Cuba's alliance with the Soviet Union and to solidify communist control of the island, precisely the result the United States was trying to avoid.
6. Lowenthal, *Dominican Intervention*, argues persuasively that the U.S. intervention exacerbated rather than attenuated the conflict and produced a political outcome that was inimical to democracy in that country.
7. Sigmund, *Overthrow of Allende*, esp. 275–92. In the context of growing U.S. public opposition to its government's policies in Vietnam and the festering Watergate scandal, the U.S. role in Chile served to galvanize Congress into hearings and initiatives to reassert its role in foreign policy. Such responses to executive branch abuses of power helped to precipitate significant shifts in foreign policy by the mid-1970s that placed much greater emphasis on human rights issues and support for democracies.
8. Schoultz, *Beneath the United States*, 332–48.
9. See, e.g., Agee, *Inside the Company*, for a detailed discussion of CIA activities in Latin America in the 1960s, Ecuador and Uruguay in particular.
10. Ameringer, *Democracy in Costa Rica*, 86, 88, 123–24.
11. U.S. government economic assistance under the Point Four program, admin-

istered by the International Cooperation Administration (ICA), totaled some $2.2 billion from the late 1940s through the 1950s. National Planning Association, "United States and Latin American Policies," 419–24. Economic development aid within the parameters of the Alliance for Progress (1961–70) came to a total of $24.7 billion, a figure that includes U.S. official development assistance, U.S. bilateral economic support, and the Agency for International Development (AID). Food for Peace (P.L. 480) assistance for the same period was an additional $1.5 billion. Hansen, "U.S.–Latin American Economic Relationships," table 10, 218–19.

12. U.S. economic assistance information for the 1970–89 period was compiled from the Foreign Commerce and Aid section of the annual *Statistical Abstract of the United States*. Total U.S. grants and credits to Latin America include aid under the Foreign Assistance Act, the Food for Peace Program (P.L. 480), and the Peace Corps.

13. For education figures, Arnove, Franz, and Morse, "Latin American Education," 124. For infant mortality, World Bank, *Social Indicators of Development*, xvi. For health and literacy data, Wilkie, *Statistical Abstract of Latin America*, sections on Health Care and Education.

14. This is what Gunnar Myrdal refers to as the "virtuous circle," in Myrdal, *Asian Drama*, vol. 3, appendix 2, 1854–55 and 1870–71.

15. Among others, Huntington, *Political Order*, esp. 1–92.

16. Palmer, "Military in Latin America," 322.

17. North American Congress on Latin America (NACLA), "U.S. Military Training Programs," 28.

18. Ibid., 25.

19. Fitch, *Armed Forces and Democracy*, esp. 12–17.

20. Palmer, "The Military in Latin America," table 2, 327.

21. Kryzanek, *U.S.–Latin American Relations*, table 8.1, 229.

22. For an overview of U.S. policy in Central America, Leogrande, *Our Own Backyard*. On Nicaragua, see Walker, *Revolution and Counterrevolution in Nicaragua*. On El Salvador, see Montgomery, *Revolution in El Salvador*.

23. On Carter's policy, see Schoultz, *Human Rights and United States Policy*, esp. 113–34, 203–10, 359–65. On the Reagan administration, see International Commission for Central American Recovery and Development, *Poverty, Conflict, and Hope*, esp. 57–66. On Panama, see Scranton, *The Noriega Years*, 185–208.

24. Diamond and Linz, "Politics, Society, and Democracy in Latin America," 1–58.

25. Inter-American Development Bank (IADB), *Economic and Social Progress in Latin America*, table 57, 424.

26. See, e.g., Roett, "Debt Crisis and Economic Development."

27. Cardoso and Dantas, "Brazil," tables 4.3 and 4.4, 130–31.

28. Williamson, ed., *Political Economy of Policy Reform*, esp. chaps. 1, 2, 5, 6, and 12.

29. Leogrande, *Our Own Backyard*, chapter 21.

30. De Soto, "International Missions and the Promotion of Peace," 1–7.

31. Menges, *Inside the National Security Council*, 96–98; Wiarda, *Finding Our Way?* 4.

32. Leogrande, *Our Own Backyard*, chapter 20, esp. 481–504.

33. Wiarda, "United States Policy in Latin America," 1–2.

34. Pastor, *Exiting the Whirlpool*, 89–92.

35. Ibid., 90.

36. Cline, *International Debt Reexamined*, 17, and table 5.3, 234–35.

37. Morici, "Grasping the Benefits of NAFTA," 49–54.

38. Pastor, *Exiting the Whirlpool*, 98–99.

39. Smith, *Talons of the Eagle*, 257–58.

40. NAFTA became operative on January 1, 1994, after the U.S. Congress ratified the treaty in November 1993, during the first year of the Clinton administration. See chapter 3 for details.

41. Hakim, "Good Neighbors Again?" 50–51.

42. Williamson, *Political Economy of Policy Reform*, 26–28.

43. Washington Office on Latin America (WOLA), *Clear and Present Dangers*, 6–20.

44. Hakim, "Good Neighbors Again?" 52.

45. Palmer, "The Often Surprising Outcomes."

46. Pastor, *Exiting the Whirlpool*, 90–92.

47. Scranton, *The Noriega Years*, 196–208.

48. Brenner, "Overcoming Asymmetry," 11.

49. Pastor, *Exiting the Whirlpool*, 101.

50. Smith, *Talons of the Eagle*, 279–80.

51. Pastor, *Exiting the Whirlpool*, 104.

Chapter 3. Latin American Policy during the Clinton Years: An Overview

1. Hakim, "The United States and Latin America," 49–53.

2. Pastor, *Exiting the Whirlpool*, 113.

3. Halberstam, *War in a Time of Peace*, 269.

4. Pastor, *Exiting the Whirlpool*, 109–10.

5. The author participated in a Department of State Bureau of Intelligence and Research briefing on Latin American issues for the new administration in May 1993 in which all the U.S. government participants except for Richard Feinberg were either Bush holdovers or prospective Clinton appointments. See also Pastor, *Exiting the Whirlpool*, 114.

6. Comment by a former senior Department of State official who asked not to be named, in a personal interview with the author, Washington, D.C., 2002. Similar sentiments were expressed by other former officials, if in less graphic terms, in personal interviews with the author.

7. Vanderbush and Haney, "Policy toward Cuba," 395–96.

8. Brian Latelle, personal interview with the author, Washington, D.C., October 4, 2001. Similar perceptions are reflected in Pezzullo, "The Leap into Haiti."

9. Pastor, *Exiting the Whirlpool*, 111.

10. Comments by "Mack" McLarty in a meeting of former Clinton administration officials at the Inter-American Dialogue in which the author participated, December 13, 2001.

11. Pastor, *Exiting the Whirlpool*, 113–14.

12. Ambassador Charles A. Gillespie Jr., personal interview with the author, Washington, D.C., February 14, 2002.

13. Smith, *The Closest of Enemies*, 210–16. Bill Clinton also attributes his reelection defeat as governor of Arkansas due to riots of Cuban prison inmates. Clinton, *My Life*, 279–83.

14. The Cuban economy declined by about 45 percent between 1989 and 1993. Smith, *Talons of the Eagle*, 321.

15. Vanderbush and Haney, "Policy toward Cuba," 397–400. See also Smith, *Talons of the Eagle*, 323–24.

16. The larger economic context that produced the peso crisis is discussed in Dominguez and Fernández, *United States and Mexico*, 61–63.

17. Pastor, *Exiting the Whirlpool*, 170.

18. Sanger, "Mexican Rescue Plan"; Rubin and Weisberg, *In an Uncertain World*, 3–38.

19. Pastor, *Exiting the Whirlpool*, 120–21; Rubin and Weisberg, *In an Uncertain World*, 34; Smith, *Talons of the Eagle*, 263–64.

20. Feinberg, *Summitry in the Americas*, 1.

21. Ibid., appendix E, 218.

22. Ibid., 161–84, and table 10.1, 165.

23. This case is discussed in more detail in chapter 4.

24. Cline, *International Debt Reexamined*, table 5.3, 234–35; Palmer, "Democracy and Its Discontents," 61.

25. Wilkie, *Statistical Abstract of Latin America*, vol. 38 (2002), table 2914, 934.

26. For U.S. investment, Wilkie, ibid., vol. 29 (1992), 1128–37, and vol. 38 (2002), 942–46. For trade, U.S. Department of Commerce, *Statistical Abstract of the United States 2001*, 802–5, and Wilkie, *Statistical Abstract of Latin America*, vol. 38 (2002), 783–90.

27. Al Matano, personal interview with the author, Washington, D.C., October 16, 2001. Assistant Secretary Matano, a 25-year Department of State veteran, noted that in his experience he had never seen an administration as pro-business as Clinton's.

28. On Nicaragua, see Lincoln and Sereseres, "Resettling the Contras"; on El Salvador, see Holiday and Stanley, "Under the Best of Circumstances."

29. Jonas, "Between Two Worlds," 92.

30. Richard Nuccio, personal interview with the author, Newport, R.I., October 30, 2001.

31. Holiday, "Guatemala's Long Road to Peace"; Jonas, "Between Two Worlds," 98–101.

32. Cameron, "Political and Economic Origins," 50–66.

33. Millett, "Central America's Enduring Conflicts," 127.

34. Valenzuela, *Collective Defense of Democracy*; Pastor, *Exiting the Whirlpool*, 302.

35. Arturo Valenzuela, personal interview with the author, Washington, D.C., October 10, 2001.

36. Inclán Oseguera, *Judicial Reform and Democratization*, esp. chapters 2 and 3.

37. Pezzullo, "The Leap into Haiti," chaps. 15 and 16, 304–53, provides details of the events leading up to the decision to withdraw the USS *Harlan County*, an explanation for the decision, and an assessment of the consequences for U.S. policy. The author is the son of Ambassador Larry Pezzullo, U.S. special advisor to Haiti between March 1993 and April 1994.

38. This case is discussed in greater detail in chapter 4.

39. Richard Nuccio, personal interview with the author, Newport, R.I., October 30, 2001; see also Vanderbush and Haney, "Policy toward Cuba," 404.

40. This case is discussed in greater detail in chapter 4.

41. Palmer, "Overcoming the Weight of History." This case is discussed in greater detail in chapter 4.

42. Ambassador Anthony C. E. Quainton, personal interview with the author, Washington, D.C., October 2, 2001.

43. Pezzullo, "The Leap into Haiti."

44. Pastor, "The Delicate Balance," 129–37.

45. Fatton, *Haiti's Predatory Republic*, 107–15.

46. Ambassador Charles A. Gillespie Jr., personal interview with the author, Washington, D.C., February 14, 2002.

47. Smith, *Talons of the Eagle*, 269.

48. The view that trade integration policy could proceed without Fast Track was articulated by some of the former Clinton officials who participated in the Inter-American Dialogue meeting with the author, and this became the subject of an extended debate there. Washington, D.C., December 13, 2001.

49. U.S. Office of National Drug Control Policy, *National Drug Control Strategy 1999*, 81.

50. David Beall, personal interview with the author, Washington, D.C., September 25, 2001.

51. For drug production information, see table 5.4.

52. Observations by Congressional Research Service (CRS) Latin American analysts in a meeting with the author, Washington, D.C., October 3, 2001.

53. Ambassador Myles Frechette, personal interview with the author, Washington, D.C., January 31, 2002.

54. Ibid. Frechette's sentiments were echoed by Ambassador Alexander Watson, personal interview with the author, Arlington, Va., October 24, 2001.

55. Ramírez Lemus, Stanton, and Walsh, "Colombia," 105–12. The Plan Colombia document is available in Bergquist et al., eds., *Violence in Colombia*, 232–39.

56. Roberts and Peceny, "Human Rights and U.S. Policy," 213–20.

57. This case is discussed in greater detail in chapter 4.

58. In his comments at the Inter-American Dialogue meeting on Latin American policy in the Clinton years with a group of officials who worked in various government offices during his administration. Washington, D.C., December 13, 2001.

59. Albright, *Madame Secretary*, 675–78.

60. Breene, *Latin American Political Yearbook 1998*, 134.

61. Pastor, *Exiting the Whirlpool*, 126.

62. Breene, *Latin American Political Yearbook 1998*, 125, 139, 143.

63. Smith, *Talons of the Eagle*, 270.

Chapter 4. Latin American Policy during the Clinton Years: Case Studies of Success and Failure

1. Ambassador Lawrence Pezzullo, in a personal interview with the author, offered his perspective on the degree of disorganization in policy discussions in the White House and within the National Security Council (NSC) during his tenure as the special advisor for Haiti in 1993 and early 1994. Baltimore, October 9, 2001. His experience with Haiti policy was confirmed for other Latin American policy issue areas over the course of the Clinton administration by the author's personal interviews with several other officials who participated in similar high-level discussions in their areas of responsibility.

2. Pastor, *Exiting the Whirlpool*, 110. This point was reinforced in a number of personal interviews by the author with U.S. government officials in the Clinton administration.

3. Martin, "Clinton Steps Up Campaign for Backing over NAFTA," 1.

4. Walsh et al., "Combatants in the Bruising NAFTA Battle," 61.

5. Turner, "President Pulled Out All the Stops," 13.

6. Garland, Harbrecht, and Dunham, "The NAFTA War Is Won," 34.

7. Turner, "President Pulled Out All the Stops," 13.

8. Lowell Fleischer, as director of the Washington office of the Council of the Americas, a New York–based organization whose membership includes most U.S. businesses with interests and/or investments in Latin America, believes that the extensive lobbying role of U.S. business on the Hill was crucial to NAFTA's ratification. E-mail communication with the author, August 1, 2005.

9. Ifill, "The Free Trade Accord," 10.

10. Rosenbaum, "The Free Trade Accord," A14.

11. Smith, *Talons of the Eagle*, 309.

12. Pastor, *Exiting the Whirlpool*, 111.

13. These concerns and issues are derived from various sources. They include Pezzullo, "The Leap into Haiti," esp. chapter 4; Ambassador Pezzullo, personal interview; Dr. Brian Latelle, former national intelligence officer for Latin America at the CIA, personal interview by the author, Washington, D.C., October 4, 2001; and Ambassador Vicki Huddleston, former deputy chief of mission at the U.S. embassy in Haiti, personal interview by the author, Cambridge, Mass., May 3, 2005.

14. Pezzullo, "The Leap into Haiti," ms., chapter 6, 166–68.

15. Ibid., chapter 8, 142–71.

16. Ibid., 307.

17. Ibid., chapter 6, esp. 155–65, and chapter 14, 286–90, 306.

18. Ibid., chapter 15, 309; Ambassador Huddleston, personal interview.

19. Pezzullo, "The Leap into Haiti," chapter 15, 316–17; Ambassador Huddleston, personal interview.

20. Pezzullo, "The Leap into Haiti," chapter 16, 329–30; Ambassador Huddleston, personal interview.

21. There is some uncertainty over just how the decision to withdraw the *Harlan County* was made and who made it. According to Ambassador Pezzulo, who attended meetings at DOS and the White House, the decision was made in the White House, but it wasn't clear if Clinton was involved. Pezzullo, "The Leap into Haiti," chapter 16, 330–36. Another account notes that "Clinton was furious and blamed his NSC staff for putting him in a lose-lose situation." Halberstam, *War in a Time of Peace*, 272. Ambassadors Pezzullo and Huddleston both noted that the president was closely involved in details of the Haitian situation and almost certainly made the decision to withdraw the *Harlan County* over the objections of DOS and Vice President Gore.

22. Ambassador Huddleston and Ambassador Pezzullo, personal interviews; Pezzullo, "The Leap into Haiti," chapter 16, 336.

23. Pezzullo, "The Leap into Haiti," chapter 12, 244–46.

24. Halberstam, *War in a Time of Peace*, 273.

25. The author first knew Dr. Pastor in this capacity in 1977 while serving as the director of Latin American and Caribbean Studies at the Foreign Service Institute of the Department of State between 1976 and 1988. On several occasions, the author and his U.S. government foreign affairs students visited NSC offices to receive classified briefings on Latin American policy issues conducted by Dr. Pastor.

26. The author conducted a personal interview with Dr. Pastor in Washington, D.C., on May 6, 2005. He is grateful to Dr. Pastor, now professor of international relations and director of the Center for Democracy and Election Management at American University, for making available numerous documents relating to his nomination.

27. Dr. Pastor, personal interview. The tension between the two presidents seems to have originated with the Mariel boat lift of Cuban refugees in 1980, when then Arkansas governor Clinton accepted the plea of President Carter to house several hundred of them at the Fort Chafee, Arkansas, military base, but then embarrassed

him when the president did not return the favor by failing to provide the federal assistance he requested when many rioted and escaped. Clinton attributed his subsequent reelection defeat in large measure to the political fall out in Arkansas from the riots. Clinton, *My Life*, 274–84.

28. Published in the *Senate Executive Report, 103–39*, 103d Cong., 2d sess., October 7, 1994, appendix N, 112–13.

29. The rough calculation of a DOS archivist consulted by H and Dr. Pastor.

30. "Additional Views of Senator Jesse Helms," *Senate Executive Report, 103–39*, 103d Cong., 2d sess., October 7, 1994, 73–74.

31. Statements by Senator Sam Nunn and Senator Alan Simpson, *Congressional Record—Senate*, 140, no. 146, S 15062-S 15063, 103d Cong., 2d sess., October 8, 1994.

32. Dr. Pastor summarizes his experience in his op-ed piece in the *Washington Post*, "Delay and Obstruct."

33. Summary drawn from "Additional Views of Senator Jesse Helms," 61–74.

34. Feinberg, *Summitry in the Americas*, 56. Ambassador Alexander Watson, then assistant secretary of state for American republics affairs, observed that he was an early proponent of a summit and discussed it with DOS and NSC officials, including Richard Feinberg. Personal interview by the author, Arlington, Va., October 24, 2001.

35. Feinberg, *Summitry in the Americas*, 53.

36. Text in ibid., appendix B, 206–7. Richard Feinberg, as senior director of inter-American affairs at the NSC, 1993–96, was the author of the original draft.

37. Ibid., 60–61.

38. Ibid., 52.

39. President Clinton's personal involvement in the decision to announce the summit proposal through Vice President Gore is confirmed by Richard Feinberg in ibid., 60–61. This version contradicts observations by several of the individuals interviewed by the author in Washington, D.C., between September and December 2001 that the president did not play a role at the outset.

40. As cited in ibid., 8–9.

41. Ibid., 9.

42. Ibid., 67–68.

43. Ibid., 72, 77.

44. Ibid., 70, and 71–80.

45. Ambassador Charles A. Gillespie, former DOS coordinator of the SOA, personal interview by the author, Washington, D.C., February 14, 2002.

46. Feinberg, *Summitry in the Americas*, 123–27, 131–32.

47. Ambassador Watson, personal interview.

48. Feinberg, *Summitry in the Americas*, appendix D, 213–17. Ambassador Watson views the articulation of these principles and their acceptance by the governments of the hemisphere as confirming the U.S. agenda for the region and its support in the region. Personal interview.

49. Feinberg, *Summitry in the Americas*, appendix E, 218–43.

50. Ibid., 84.

51. Ambassador Gillespie, personal interview.

52. Feinberg, *Summitry in the Americas*, 101–2. As suggested here by Feinberg, the OAS was viewed as primarily a debate forum that lacked the capacity needed to effectively track Summit implementation. Several other U.S. officials the author interviewed shared this view, even though some of them still disagreed with the decision not to use the OAS for follow-up coordination.

53. Although Feinberg, in ibid., 161–84, acknowledges some of the difficulties in implementation inherent in the complex follow-up arrangements, his assessment of progress is more positive than the author's, who found, in a 1996 search of about a dozen of the contact points for information on post-summit advances, only one that was actually functioning at that point in time.

54. Ibid., 97.

55. Ibid., 177.

56. Among others, St. John, "Las relaciones Ecuador-Perú," 90–104.

57. Palmer, "Overcoming the Weight of History," 40, 46n32.

58. Palmer, "Peru-Ecuador Border Conflict," 118, 135–37, 141n11.

59. Ambassador Watson, personal interview.

60. Weidner, "Peacekeeping," 53–57.

61. Ambassador Watson, personal interview.

62. Ambassador Einaudi provides his own account in "The Ecuador-Peru Peace Process."

63. For a fuller account of the process and its ultimately successful outcome, see Palmer, "Overcoming the Weight of History," 32–44.

64. Vanderbush and Haney, "Policy toward Cuba," 394–95.

65. Pastor, *Exiting the Whirlpool*, 119.

66. Vanderbush and Haney, "Policy toward Cuba," 407.

67. Ibid., 402.

68. Brenner, "Overcoming Asymmetry," 7.

69. Vanderbush and Haney, "Policy toward Cuba," 403–4; Nuccio, "Unmaking Cuba Policy," 4–5.

70. Vanderbush and Haney, "Policy toward Cuba," 404.

71. Ibid., 405.

72. Ibid.

73. Dom, "La política de Estados Unidos hacia Cuba," 11–13; Nuccio, "Unmaking Cuba Policy," 3.

74. Palmer, "Peru, the Drug Business, and Shining Path," 66–74.

75. Palmer, "'Fujipopulism' and Peru's Progress," 70–72.

76. McClintock and Vallas, *The United States and Peru*, 142–47.

77. Washington Office on Latin America (WOLA), "Drug War Paradoxes," 1–5.

78. Ambassador Anthony C. E. Quainton, personal interview with the author, Washington, D.C., October 2, 2001.

79. McClintock and Vallas, *The United States and Peru*, 87–88.

80. Ambassador Dennis Jett, personal interviews by the author, Lima, Peru, July 31, 1998, and July 1, 1999.

81. Ambassador John Hamilton, personal interview by the author, Lima, Peru, January 18, 2000.

82. At a forum on the upcoming elections cosponsored by Transparencia and the National Democratic Institute in Lima, Peru, attended by the author, January 18, 2000.

83. As an OAS electoral observer sent to Chiclayo for Peru's 2000 election, the author witnessed firsthand computer manipulation of voting results in this region after they had been compiled and sent to Lima. The author, having returned to Lima to help prepare the final regional report, also viewed the various protests by important international figures on the only television station reporting them and saw at close hand the impact they had on government and opposition alike. Following these statements, Fujimori officials pulled back almost immediately from their projections of first-round victory, and 10 of the 11 opposition party presidential candidates joined forces to lead a significant popular protest. April 3–12, 2000.

84. McClintock and Vallas, *The United States and Peru*, 153.

85. Balbi and Palmer, "'Reinventing' Democracy in Peru," 68–72.

86. Ambassador Viron P. Vaky, personal interview by the author, Washington, D.C., September 19, 2001.

87. Various former and current DOS officials, both in Washington and in Latin America, reflected on this problem in personal interviews with the author. Several contrasted this experience during the Clinton administration with that under his predecessor, where Assistant Secretary Bernard Aronson enjoyed the confidence of Secretary of State Howard Baker, who, like his successors under Clinton, had no particular interest in Latin America. Such confidence and a hands-off management style gave Aronson the latitude he needed to formulate and follow through on policies toward the region.

88. Col. Jay Cope (Ret.), personal interview with the author, Washington, D.C., October 3, 2001.

Chapter 5. Latin American Policy during the Clinton Years: An Assessment

1. Freedom House, *Freedom in the World: Country Ratings 1972 through 2003.*

2. *Latin American Weekly Report*, April 26, 2005, 3. The latest example, in Bolivia, occurred after publication of this summary of unorthodox regime changes.

3. U.S. General Accounting Office, *Foreign Assistance*, 61, 63.

4. Among a number of critical analyses of the U.S. drug policy is Bertram et al., *Drug War Politics*. A historical overview of the issue may be found in Walker, ed., *Drugs in the Western Hemisphere.*

5. See table 5.2 source for annual Political Rights and Civil Liberties scaling. Many analysts, including those cited in note 4 above, argue that the U.S. supply-oriented counter-drug policy in Latin America cannot be successful as long as U.S. consumer

demand for cocaine and heroin remains high, and that the policy has a significant negative impact on democratic governance in the affected countries. Their argument that the policy should be abandoned, however, runs counter to U.S. domestic political realities, especially among elected officials who want to be seen as forceful on the drug issue, making any major adjustment to the policy unlikely.

6. Ambassador Charles Gillespie Jr. noted that the trade issue was only 1 of 2 not decided among the 23 initiatives to be on the agenda of the SOA at the preparatory meeting held at Airlie House in Warrenton, Virginia, just days before the summit. He attributed the lack of agreement on trade to differences between White House policy and political advisors and within the Office of the Trade Representative (OTR), resolved only at the last minute by the decision of OTR director Charlene Barshevsky. Gillespie was serving at the time as the coordinator for the SOA meeting. Personal interview with the author, Washington, D.C., February 14, 2002.

7. Pastor, *Exiting the Whirlpool*, 131.

8. The figures for other years were 5.8 percent in 1994, 6.7 percent in 1997, and 9.0 percent in 2002. United Nations Economic Commission for Latin America and the Caribbean (ECLAC), *Social Panorama of Latin America*, table III.5a, 158.

9. Smith, *Talons of the Eagle*, 279–80.

10. Ibid., 280–82; Gallagher, *Free Trade and the Environment*, 72–79.

11. Ambassador Alexander Watson, personal interview with the author, Arlington, Va., October 24, 2001.

12. United Nations Environment Program, *Global Environmental Outlook*, 54.

13. Ibid., 60–61.

14. Gallagher, *Free Trade and the Environment*, 74–79.

15. Such concerns were expressed by a number of U.S. government officials in personal interviews with the author in Washington, D.C., in 2001 and 2002, particularly among Foreign Service officers and midlevel Civil Service employees in the Department of State.

16. The Consumer Price Index (CPI) increased by 19 percent between 1988 and 1992 and by 23 percent between 1992 and 2000. U.S. Department of Commerce, *Statistical Abstract 2002*, table 681, 451.

17. DOS employment in 1994 was 25,596 and in 1996, 24,489. USIA had 7,888 employees in 1994 and 6,850 in 1996, while USAID went from 4,059 in 1994 to 3,267 two years later. U.S. Department of Commerce, *Statistical Abstract 1997*, table 536, 348.

18. Bacchus, *Price of American Foreign Policy*, 11–21.

Interviews with Former Clinton Administration Officials, U.S. Government Personnel, and Foreign Policy Analysts

David Beall, executive director, Inter-American Drug Abuse Control Commission, Organization of American States (OAS). Washington, D.C., September 25, 2001.

Guillermo Belt, career OAS official, retired. Washington, D.C., October 16, 2001.

Barbara Bowie-Whitcomb, economic officer, U.S. delegation to the OAS, 1993–96. Washington, D.C., September 26, 2001.

James Buchanan, director for South America, Bureau of Intelligence and Research, State Department. Washington, D.C., October 1, 2001.

Sean Carroll, coordinator for congressional affairs, Inter-American Dialogue (IAD). Washington, D.C., October 4, 2001.

Jay Cope, colonel, U.S. Army (ret.), National Defense University. Washington, D.C., October 3, 2001.

Peter De Shazo, deputy director, U.S. mission to the OAS. Washington, D.C., October 24, 2001.

Miles Frechette, U.S. ambassador to Colombia, 1994–98. Washington, D.C., January 31, 2002.

Charles A. Gillespie Jr., U.S. ambassador to Chile, 1990–92, senior director for Western Hemisphere affairs, National Security Council (NSC), 1992–93, coordinator, Summit of the Americas, 1994. Washington, D.C., February 14, 2002.

Peter Hakim, president, IAD. Washington, D.C., August 29, 2001; October 17, 2001; December 18, 2001.

John Hamilton, U.S. Ambassador to Peru, 1999–2001. Lima, Peru, January 18, 2000.

Margaret Daly Hayes, director, Institute for Hemispheric Security, National Defense University. Washington, D.C., October 17, 2001.

Vicki Huddleston, chargé d'affaires, U.S. embassy, Haiti, 1993. Cambridge, Mass., May 3, 2005.

Dennis Jett, U.S. Ambassador to Peru, 1997–99. Lima, Peru, July 31, 1998; July 1, 1999.

Brian Latelle, deputy director, Latin America Office, Central Intelligence Agency. Washington, D.C., October 4, 2001.

Al Matano, assistant secretary, Bureau of International Narcotics and Legal Affairs, State Department. Washington, D.C., October 16, 2001.

Cynthia McClintock, professor and director of Latin American studies, George Washington University. Washington, D.C., October 12, 2001.

Richard Nuccio, senior policy advisor, State Department, 1995–97. Newport, R.I., October 30, 2001.

David Passage, director, Office of Andean Affairs, State Department, 1996–99. Arlington, Va., September 26, 2001; December 12, 2001.

Robert Pastor, fellow, Carter Center, 1990–95. Washington, D.C., May 6, 2005.

Larry Pezzullo, U.S. special advisor to Haiti, 1993–94. Baltimore, October 9, 2001.

Anthony C. E. Quainton, U.S. ambassador to Peru, 1989–92, assistant secretary for international security, 1994–95, director general of the Foreign Service, 1995–97. Washington, D.C., October 2, 2001.

Riordan Roett, professor and director of Latin American studies, School of Advanced International Studies, Johns Hopkins University. Washington, D.C., October 10, 2001.

Nina Serafino, Congressional Research Service (CRS). Washington, D.C., October 3, 2001.

Michael Shifter, vice president for policy, IAD. Washington, D.C., September 13, 2001; October 24, 2001; December 20, 2001.

Michael Southwick, special advisor to Secretary of State Colin Powell, 2001–3. Washington, D.C., January 31, 2002.

Larry Storrs, CRS. Washington, D.C., October 3, 2001.

Mark Sullivan, CRS. Washington, D.C., October 3, 2001.

Joseph Tulchin, director for Latin America, Woodrow Wilson Center. Washington, D.C., October 1, 2001.

Viron P. Vaky, senior fellow, IAD. Washington, D.C., September 19, 2001; December 12, 2001.

Arturo Valenzuela, deputy assistant secretary of state, Bureau of Inter-American Affairs, State Department, 1994–96; senior director for Western Hemisphere Affairs, NSC, 1998–2000. Washington, D.C., October 10, 2001.

George Vickers, director, Washington Office on Latin America (WOLA); director, Open Society Institute, 1998–. Washington, D.C., February 21, 2002.

Alexander Watson, assistant secretary of state, Bureau of Inter-American Affairs, State Department, 1993–96. Arlington, Va., October 24, 2001.

Robert White, director, Center for International Policy. Washington, D.C., October 24, 2001.

In addition to the individual interviews and conversations noted above, the Inter-American Dialogue sponsored two closed meetings of senior Clinton administration officials to review and assess Latin American and Caribbean policies during the Clinton years. These were held on December 13, 2001, and on February 21, 2002. The following individuals attended:

December 13, 2001

Lael Brainard, deputy national economic advisor and deputy assistant to President Clinton for International Economic Affairs.

Georges Fauriol, director, International Republican Institute.

Jon Huenemann, Office of the U.S. Trade Representative (USTR).

Michelle Manatt, director of legislative affairs, Office of National Drug Control Policy, State Department.

Thomas F. McLarty, White House chief of staff, counselor to the president, and special envoy for the Americas, 1993–98.

Larry Pezzullo, special advisor to Haiti, 1993–94.

Ted Piccone, associate director, Latin America Office, Defense Department, 1993–95.

Mark Schneider, director for Latin America, U.S. Agency for International Development (USAID), 1993–99; director, Peace Corps, 1999–2001.

Michael Shifter, IAD.

Viron P. Vaky, IAD.

Arturo Valenzuela, deputy assistant secretary, Bureau of Inter-American Affairs, State Department; senior director, Western Hemisphere Affairs, NSC.

February 21, 2002

Harriet Babbitt, ambassador to the OAS, 1993–97.

Jane Bussey, reporter, *Miami Herald.*

Robert Gelbard, U.S. ambassador to Bolivia, 1989–92; director, Office of International Narcotics and Legal Affairs, State Department, 1993–97.

Peter Hakim, IAD.

Jon Huenemann, Office of the U.S. Trade Representative.

Rich Klein, assistant to Thomas McLarty.

Kenneth McCay, White House advisor to President Clinton, 1997–2001.

John O'Leary, U.S. ambassador to Chile, 1998–2001.

Pedro Pablo Permuy, staff assistant, Western Hemisphere Subcommittee, U.S. House of Representatives.

Ted Piccone, Defense Department.

Peter Romero, U.S. ambassador to Ecuador, 1995–98; assistant secretary for Western Hemisphere affairs, State Department, 1999–2001.

Bibliography

Agee, Philip. *Inside the Company: CIA Diary*. Harmondsworth: Penguin Books, 1975.

Albright, Madeleine. *Madam Secretary: A Memoir*. New York: Hyperion, 2003.

Allison, Graham T. *Essence of Decision: Explaining the Cuban Missile Crisis*. Boston: Little, Brown, 1971.

Ameringer, Charles D. *Democracy in Costa Rica*. New York: Praeger, 1982.

Arnove, Robert F., Stephen Franz, and Kimberley Morse. "Latin American Education." In *Latin America: Perspectives on a Region*. 2d ed., ed. Jack W. Hopkins, 123–37. New York: Holmes and Meier, 1998.

Bacchus, William I. *The Price of American Foreign Policy Congress, the Executive, and International Affairs Funding*. University Park: Pennsylvania State University Press, 1997.

Balbi, Carmen Rosa, and David Scott Palmer, "'Reinventing' Democracy in Peru." *Current History* 100, no. 643 (February 2001): 65–72.

Bergquist, Charles, Ricardo Peñaranda, and Gonzalo Sánchez G., eds. *Violence in Colombia, 1990–2000: Waging War and Negotiating Peace*. Wilmington, Del.: Scholarly Resources Books, 2001.

Bertram, Eva, Morris Blachman, Kenneth Sharpe, and Peter Andreas. *Drug War Politics: The Price of Denial*. Berkeley: University of California Press, 1996.

Breene, Robert, Jr. *Latin American Political Yearbook 1998*. New Brunswick, N.J.: Transaction, 1999.

Brenner, Philip. "Overcoming Asymmetry: The Meaning of U.S.–Cuban Relations for U.S. Policy towards Latin America." Paper prepared for delivery at the 25th International Congress of the Latin American Studies Association, Las Vegas, October 7–9, 2004.

Cameron, Maxwell A. "Political and Economic Origins of Regime Change in Peru: The *Eighteenth Brumaire* of Alberto Fujimori." In *The Peruvian Labyrinth: Polity, Society, Economy*, ed. Maxwell Cameron and Philip Mauceri, 37–69. University Park: Pennsylvania State University Press, 1997.

Cardoso, Eliana, and Daniel Dantas. "Brazil." In *Latin American Adjustment: How Much Has Happened?* ed. John Williamson, 129–53. Washington, D.C.: Institute for International Economics, 1990.

Cline, William R. *International Debt Reexamined*. Washington, D.C.: Institute for International Economics, 1995.

Clinton, Bill. *My Life*. New York: Knopf, 2004.

de Soto, Álvaro. "International Missions and the Promotion of Peace and Democracy." In *Peacemaking and Democratization in the Western Hemisphere*, ed. Tommie Sue Montgomery, 1–7. Miami: North-South Center Press at the University of Miami, 2000.

Diamond, Larry, and Juan J. Linz. "Introduction: Politics, Society, and Democracy in Latin America." In *Democracy in Developing Countries: Latin America*, ed. Larry Diamond, Juan J. Linz, and Seymour Martin Lipset, 1–58. Boulder, Colo.: Lynne Rienner, 1989.

Dom, Jorge. "La política de Estados Unidos hacia Cuba durante la segunda presidencia de Clinton." Working Papers on Latin America series. Cambridge: David Rockefeller Center for Latin American Studies, Harvard University, 2001.

Dominguez, Jorge I., and Rafael Fernández de Castro. *The United States and Mexico: Between Partnership and Conflict*. New York: Routledge, 2001.

Einaudi, Luigi R. "The Ecuador-Peru Peace Process." In *Herding Cats: Multiparty Mediation in a Complex World*, ed. Chester A. Crocker, Fen Osler Hampson, and Pamela Aall, 407–29. Washington, D.C.: United Institute of Peace Press, 1999.

Fatton, Robert, Jr. *Haiti's Predatory Republic: The Unending Transition to Democracy*. Boulder, Colo.: Lynne Rienner, 2002.

Feinberg, Richard E. *Summitry in the Americas: A Progress Report*. Washington, D.C.: Institute for International Economics, 1997.

Fitch, J. Samuel. *The Armed Forces and Democracy in Latin America*. Baltimore: Johns Hopkins University Press, 1998.

Freedom House. *Freedom in the World 2003: Survey Methodology*, <freedomhouse.org/research/freeworld/2003/methodology.htm> (July 23, 2005).

———. *Freedom in the World: Country Ratings 1972 through 2003*. <freedomhouse.org/ratings/allscore04.xls> (July 22, 2005).

Gallagher, Kevin P. *Free Trade and the Environment: Mexico, NAFTA, and Beyond*. Stanford Law and Politics. Stanford: Stanford University Press, 2004.

Garland, Susan B., Douglas Harbrecht, and Richard S. Dunham. "The NAFTA War Is Won. Now Clinton Must Mend Fences." *Business Week*, no. 3348: 34.

Gorriti, Gustavo. "La CIA y Montesinos." *Ideele, Revista del Instituto de Defensa Legal*, no. 162 (April 2004): 12–17.

Hakim, Peter. "The United States and Latin America: Good Neighbors Again?" *Current History* 91, no. 562 (February 1992): 50–53.

Halberstam, David. *War in a Time of Peace: Bush, Clinton, and the Generals*. New York: Scribner, 2001.

Hansen, Roger. "U.S.–Latin American Economic Relationships: Bilateral, Regional, or Global?" In *The Americas in a Changing World: A Report of the Commission on United States–Latin American Relations*, 196–238. New York: New York Times Book Company, 1975.

Holiday, David. "Guatemala's Long Road to Peace." *Current History* 96, no. 607 (February 1997): 68–74.

Holiday, David, and William Stanley. "Under the Best of Circumstances: ONUSAL and the Challenges of Verification and Institution Building in El Salvador." In *Peacemaking and Democratization in the Western Hemisphere*, ed. Tammie Sue Montgomery, 37–66. Miami: North-South Center Press at the University of Miami, 2000.

Huntington, Samuel P. *Political Order in Changing Societies*. New Haven: Yale University Press, 1968.

———. *The Third Wave: Democratization in the Late Twentieth Century*. Norman: University of Oklahoma Press, 1991.

Ifill, Gwen. "The Free Trade Accord: Clinton Extends an Unusual Offer to Republicans on the Pact." *New York Times* (November 13, 1993): 10.

Immerman, Richard H. *The CIA in Guatemala: The Foreign Policy of Intervention*. Austin: University of Texas Press, 1982.

Inclán Oseguera, Silvia. *Judicial Reform and Democratization: Mexico in the 1990s*. Ph.D. diss., Boston University, 2003.

Inter-American Development Bank, *Economic and Social Progress in Latin America: External Debt, Crisis and Adjustment*. Washington, D.C.: Inter-American Development Bank, 1985.

International Commission for Central American Recovery and Development. *Poverty, Conflict, and Hope: A Turning Point in Central America*. Durham, N.C.: Duke University Press, 1989.

Jonas, Suzanne. "Between Two Worlds: The United Nations in Guatemala." In *Peacemaking and Democratization in the Western Hemisphere*, ed. Tommie Sue Montgomery, 91–106. Miami: North-South Center Press at the University of Miami, 2000.

Kennan, George. "Latin America as a Problem in United States Foreign Policy." In *Neighborly Adversaries: Readings in U.S.–Latin American Relations*, ed. Michael La Rosa and Frank O. Mora, 177–88. Lanham, Md.: Rowman and Littlefield, 1999.

Kryzanek, Michael J. *U.S.–Latin American Relations*. 3d ed. Westport, Conn.: Praeger, 1996.

Leogrande, William M. *Our Own Backyard: The United States in Central America, 1977–1992*. Chapel Hill: University of North Carolina Press, 1998.

Lincoln, Jennie K., and César Sereseres. "Resettling the Contras: The OAS Verification Commission in Nicaragua." In *Peacemaking and Democratization in the Western Hemisphere*, ed. Tommie Sue Montgomery, 17–36. Miami: North-South Center Press at the University of Miami, 2000.

Lowenthal, Abraham F. *The Dominican Intervention*. Cambridge: Harvard University Press, 1972.

Martin, Jurek. "Clinton Steps Up Campaign for Backing over NAFTA: President Accuses Unions of 'Roughshod' Tactics on Free Trade Agreement." *Financial Times* (November 8, 1993): 1.

McClintock, Cynthia, and Fabian Vallas. *The United States and Peru: Cooperation at a Cost*. New York: Routledge, 2003.

Menges, Constantine C. *Inside the National Security Council: The True Story of the Making and Unmaking of Reagan's Foreign Policy*. New York: Simon and Schuster, 1988.

Millett, Richard L. "Central America's Enduring Conflicts." *Current History* 93, no. 581 (March 1994): 124–28.

Milner, Helen. *Interests, Institutions, and Information.* Princeton: Princeton University Press, 1997.

Montgomery, Tommie Sue. *Revolution in El Salvador: From Civil Strife to Civil Peace.* 2d ed. Boulder, Colo.: Westview Press, 1995.

Morganthau, Hans. *Politics among Nations: The Struggle for Power and Peace* New York: Knopf, 1967.

Morici, Peter, "Grasping the Benefits of NAFTA." *Current History* 92, no. 571 (February 1993): 49–54.

Myrdal, Gunnar. *Asian Drama: An Inquiry into the Poverty of Nations.* Vol. 3. New York: Pantheon, 1968.

National Planning Association. "United States and Latin American Policies Affecting Their Economic Relations." In *United States–Latin American Relations: Compilation of Studies,* Subcommittee on American Republics Affairs of the Committee on Foreign Relations, U.S. Senate, 399–537. Washington, D.C.: Government Printing Office, 1960.

North American Congress on Latin America (NACLA). "U.S. Military Training Programs for Foreign Military Personnel." *Latin America and Empire Report* 10, no. 1 (January 1976): 24–31.

Nuccio, Richard A. "Unmaking Cuba Policy: The Clinton Years." *Foreign Service Journal* (October 1998): 1–7.

Office of National Drug Control Policy, *National Drug Control Strategy 1999.* Washington, D.C.: Government Printing Office, 2000.

Palmer, David Scott. "Democracy and Its Discontents in Fujimori's Peru." *Current History* 99, no. 634 (February 2000): 60–65.

———. "Fujipopulism and Peru's Progress." *Current History* 95, no. 598 (February 1996): 70–75.

———. "The Military in Latin America." In *Latin America: Perspectives on a Region,* 2d ed., ed. Jack W. Hopkins, 320–37. New York: Holmes and Meier, 1998.

———. "The Often Surprising Outcomes of Asymmetry in International Affairs: United States–Peru Relations in the 1990s." In *The Fujimori Legacy,* ed. Julio Carrion, 227–41. University Park: Pennsylvania State University Press, 2006.

———. "Overcoming the Weight of History: 'Getting to Yes' in the Peru-Ecuador Border Dispute." *Diplomacy and Statecraft* 12, no. 2 (June 2001): 29–46.

———. "Peru, the Drug Business, and Shining Path: Between Scylla and Charybdis?" *Journal of Interamerican Studies and World Affairs* 34, no. 3 (Fall 1992): 65–88.

———. "Peru-Ecuador Border Conflict: Missed Opportunities, Misplaced Nationalism, and Multilateral Peacekeeping." *Journal of Interamerican Studies and World Affairs* 39, no. 3 (Fall 1997): 109–48.

Pastor, Robert A. "Delay and Obstruct: My Nomination Is Dead and Jesse Helms Is Still Fighting the Panama Canal Treaties." *Washington Post* (February 1, 1995): 23.

———. "The Delicate Balance between Coercion and Diplomacy: The Case of Haiti, 1994." In *The United States and Coercive Diplomacy*, ed. Robert J. Art and Patrick M. Cronin, 119–55. Washington, D.C.: U.S. Institute of Peace Press, 2003.

———. *Exiting the Whirlpool: U.S. Foreign Policy toward Latin America and the Caribbean.* 2d ed. Boulder, Colo.: Westview Press, 2001.

Peeler, John. *Building Democracy in Latin America.* 2d ed. Boulder, Colo.: Lynne Rienner, 2004.

Pezzullo, Ralph. "The Leap into Haiti; or, How Not to Conduct U.S. Foreign Policy in the Post Cold War." Manuscript, 2001. Forthcoming as *Plunging into Haiti: Clinton, Aristide, and the Defeat of Diplomacy.* Jackson, Miss.: University Press of Mississippi, 2006.

Putnam, Robert. "Diplomacy and Domestic Politics: The Logic of Two-Level Games." *International Organization* 42, no. 3 (Summer 1988): 427–60.

Ramírez Lemus, María Clemencia, Kimberley Stanton, and John Walsh. "Colombia: A Vicious Circle of Drugs and War." In *Drugs and Democracy in Latin America: The Impact of U.S. Policy*, ed. Coletta A. Youngers and Eileen Rosin, 99–142. Boulder, Colo.: Lynne Rienner, 2005.

Roberts, Kenneth, and Mark Peceny. "Human Rights and United States Policy toward Peru." In *The Peruvian Labyrinth: Polity, Society, Economy*, ed. Maxwell A. Cameron and Philip Mauceri, 192–222. University Park: Pennsylvania State University Press, 1997.

Roett, Riordan. "The Debt Crisis and Economic Development in Latin America." In *The United States and Latin America in the 1990s: Beyond the Cold War*, ed. Jonathan Hartlyn, Lars Schoultz, and Augusto Varas, 131–51. Chapel Hill: University of North Carolina Press, 1992.

Rosenbaum, David. "The Free Trade Accord: Both Sides Emphasize High Stakes of Trade Vote." *New York Times* (November 15, 1993): A14.

Rubin, Robert E., and Jacob Weisberg. *In an Uncertain World: Tough Choices from Wall Street to Washington.* New York: Random House, 2004.

Sanger, David E. "Mexican Rescue Plan: The Overview." *New York Times* (February 1, 1995): 1+.

Schlesinger, Stephen, and Stephen Kinzer. *Bitter Fruit: The Untold Story of the American Coup in Guatemala.* Garden City, N.Y.: Doubleday, 1982.

Schoultz, Lars. *Beneath the United States: A History of U.S. Policy toward Latin America.* Cambridge: Harvard University Press, 1998.

———. *Human Rights and United States Policy toward Latin America.* Princeton: Princeton University Press, 1981.

Scranton, Margaret E. *The Noriega Years: U.S.–Panamanian Relations, 1981–1990.* Boulder, Colo.: Lynne Rienner, 1991.

Sigmund, Paul A. *The Overthrow of Allende and the Politics of Chile, 1964–1976.* Pittsburgh: University of Pittsburgh Press, 1977.

Smith, Peter H. *Democracy in Latin America: Political Change in Comparative Perspective.* New York: Oxford University Press, 2005.

————. *Talons of the Eagle: Dynamics of U.S.–Latin American Relations.* 2d ed. New York: Oxford University Press, 2000.

Smith, Wayne S. *The Closest of Enemies: A Personal and Diplomatic History of the Castro Years.* New York: W. W. Norton, 1987.

St. John, Ronald Bruce. "Las relaciones Ecuador-Peru: una perspective histórica." In *Ecuador-Perú: Horizontes de la negociación y el conflicto,* ed. Adrián Bonilla, 89–110. Quito: FLACSO, Sede Ecuador, 1999.

Transparency International. *Corruption Perceptions Index.* Annual, 1995–2002. <www.transparency.org/cpi.en.html> (July 22, 2005).

Turner, Douglas. "President Pulled Out All the Stops for Huge Victory on NAFTA." *Buffalo News* (November 21, 1993): 13.

United Nations Economic Commission for Latin America and the Caribbean. *Social Panorama of Latin America 2002–2003.* UN Pub. LC/G. 2209-P. Santiago, Chile: UN Publications, May 2004.

————. *A Decade of Light and Shadow: Latin America and the Caribbean in the 1990s,* ed. José Antonio Ocampo and Juan Martin. Santiago, Chile: ECLAC, July 2003.

United Nations Environment Program (UNEP). *Global Environmental Outlook: Latin America and the Caribbean—2003.* San José, Costa Rica: UNEP, November 2003. <www.mirror.unep.org/geo/pdfs/GEO_lac2003English.pdf> (August 7, 2005).

U.S. Department of Commerce. *Statistical Abstract of the United States.* Washington, D.C.: Government Printing Office, annual. <www.census.gov/prod/www/abs/statab1951-1994.htm> (accessed August 14, 2005).

U.S. General Accounting Office (USGAO). *Foreign Assistance: U.S. Democracy Programs in Six Latin American Countries Have Yielded Modest Results.* GAO-03-358. Washington, D.C.: USGAO, March 2003. <www.gao.gov/new.items/d03358.pdf> (July 18, 2005).

U.S. Office of National Drug Control Policy. *National Drug Control Strategy 1999.* Washington, D.C.: Government Printing Office, 2000.

Urrego, Miguel Ángel. "Social and Popular Movements in a Time of Cholera, 1977–1999." In *Violence in Colombia, 1990–2000: Waging War and Negotiating Peace,* ed. Charles Bergquist, Ricardo Peñaranda, and Gonzalo Sánchez G., 171–78. Wilmington, Del.: Scholarly Resources Books, 2001.

Valenzuela, Arturo. *The Collective Defense of Democracy: Lessons from the Paraguayan Crisis of 1996.* Report to the Carnegie Commission on Preventing Deadly Conflict. New York: Carnegie, 1999.

Vanderbush, Walt, and Patrick J. Haney. "Policy toward Cuba in the Clinton Administration." *Political Science Quarterly* 114, no. 3: 387–408.

Walker, Thomas W. *Revolution and Counterrevolution in Nicaragua.* Boulder, Colo.: Westview Press, 1991.

Walker, William O., III, ed. *Drugs in the Western Hemisphere: An Odyssey of Cultures in Conflict.* Jaguar Books on Latin America, no. 12. Wilmington, Del.: Scholarly Resources Books, 1996.

Walsh, Kenneth T., David Hage, Jim Impoco, and Linda Robinson. "Combatants in the Bruising NAFTA Battle Begin to Dig In Their Heels." *U.S. News and World Report* 115, no. 10: 61.

Washington Office on Latin America (WOLA). "Drug War Paradoxes: The U.S. Government and Peru's Vladimir Montesinos." *Drug War Monitor,* a WOLA Briefing Series. Washington, D.C.: WOLA, July 2004.

———. *Clear and Present Dangers: The U.S. Military and the War on Drugs in the Andes.* Washington, D.C.: WOLA, 1991.

Weidner, Glenn R. "Peacekeeping in the Upper Cenepa Valley: A Regional Response to Crisis." In *Security Cooperation in the Western Hemisphere: Resolving the Ecuador-Peru Conflict,* ed. Gabriel Marcella and Richard Downes, 45–66. Miami: North-South Center Press at the University of Miami, 1999.

Wiarda, Howard J. "United States Policy in Latin America." *Current History* 89, no. 543 (January 1990): 1–8, 31.

———. Finding Our Way? Toward Maturity in U.S.–Latin American Relations. Washington, D.C. American Enterprise Institute for Public Policy Research, 1987.

Wilkie, James W., ed. *Statistical Abstract of Latin America.* Vols. 18, 29, 38. Los Angeles: UCLA Latin American Center, 1977, 1992, 2002.

Williamson, John, ed. *The Political Economy of Policy Reform.* Washington, D.C.: Institute for International Economics, 1993.

Wittkopf, Eugene R. *The Domestic Sources of American Foreign Policy: Insights and Evidence.* 2d ed. New York: St. Martin's Press, 1994.

Wood, Bryce. *The Dismantling of the Good Neighbor Policy.* Austin: University of Texas Press, 1985.

World Bank. *Social Indicators of Development, 1991–92.* Baltimore: Johns Hopkins University Press, 1992.

Youngers, Coletta A., and Eileen Rosin, "The U.S. 'War on Drugs': Its Impact in Latin America and the Caribbean." In *Drugs and Democracy in Latin America: The Impact of U.S. Policy,* ed. Coletta A. Youngers and Eileen Rosin, 1–14. Boulder, Colo.: Lynne Rienner, 2005.

Index

David Scott Palmer is professor of international relations and political science at Boston University. Before coming to his present position, he served for twelve years as director of Latin American and Caribbean studies at the Foreign Service Institute of the U.S. Department of State, where he was also coordinator for the advanced area studies program and associate dean for programs in the School of Area Studies. He consults with the Department of State, the National Intelligence Council, and the U.S. Agency for International Development on policy issues related to terrorism, conflict resolution, and problems of democracy in Latin America. He lectures widely at colleges and universities in the United States, Latin America, and Spain on these and other topics, and is the author of books on Latin American politics and articles on United States–Latin American relations, among other subjects.

CPSIA information can be obtained
at www.ICGtesting.com
Printed in the USA
BVOW08s2223200717
489881BV00002B/43/P